CW01468442

The Wonder
My Life & Times With Stevie Wonder

Ted Hull
with Paula L. Stahel

Copyright 2000 © Ted Hull

ISBN 0-9720644-0-0

Published by Ted Hull, Tampa FL.

All rights reserved. No part of this publication may be reproduced, stored in a retrieval system, or transmitted, in any form or by any means, electronic, mechanical, photocopying, recording, or otherwise, without the prior written permission of the copyright holder.

Second Edition

PRINTED IN THE UNITED STATES OF AMERICA

Booklocker.com, Inc.
2002

Dedicated to my sons,
Ted Cordell and Robert John,
each of whom was named for a man of peace.

Acknowledgments

Finally, the book's finished. But it looks so slender when compared to the time work effort that went into it. When I first started writing the manuscript, I thought it would take about a year. It took many times that.

Over the years I've noticed that most married authors thank their wives profusely. Now I understand why. When the going really got tough, there was no one else to turn to. Margaret, thanks for everything.

I have relied heavily on my memory and the memory of others. We all learn that with the years that go by—and, in this case, many years—the memory sometimes becomes a little shrouded. If in these pages I have erred or in some way offended anyone, I apologize and am willing to make corrections in future printings. I never thought I could do this book by myself, and in that I was right. I owe a lot of gratitude to some very special people.

First, I would like to thank Beans Bowles. Beans was a Motown musician and worked in the talent management department. He was one of the original Motown employees and managed many of the Motown reviews that Stevie and I were a part of. He also played flute on the studio version of *Fingertips*—Stevie's first chart-topping hit. Hank Cosby, songwriter/producer, worked with all the great Motown artists at one time or another. He also co-wrote and produced *Uptight*, the song that got Stevie back on top of the charts. Clarence Paul, Stevie's first producer and musical director, traveled with us in the early years and is generally thought of as being very influential in Stevie's early, formidable years as a musician and entertainer. And then there was Gene Shelby, our drive and Stevie's loyal valet. I fondly remember Gene driving us to the airport at 100 miles and hour, and chasing women in his spare time. All of these men were at Motown when Stevie arrived on the scene. They told me many fascinating stories of those early days and helped me better remember our years together. They all were loved and respected by "Little Stevie Wonder."

The very first person I met at Motown Record Company was Esther Gordy Edwards, who at the time, was Senior Vice President and is presently the Founding Director of the Motown Historical Museum in Detroit. It was Esther who encouraged me to write this book. We spent hours together with my tape recorder, resurrecting old memories. Her on-going encouragement has been extremely valuable to this day. She is truly a unique individual who touched the lives of many artists in the Motown stables.

Having a story to tell is one thing. Getting it on paper and in a reasonable format for editing is, for me, a big problem. I recognize that my lack of good vision requires assistance sometimes, but in some things I'm just plain stupid. Thank goodness I had Equilla Brooks, Debbie Moore and Meg Ames to turn to for reading the manuscript to me, over and over, so that I could do the first crude editing and rewrites, typing, collating, mailing and the many other office-type things that I don't do well. Along the way there were many editorial suggestions that were very helpful.

Jackie and Preston Trigg did me a big favor when they introduced me to Ace Atkins, author of *Leavin' Trunk Blues* and *Crossroads Blues*. His encouragement and knowledge of the publishing industry were especially beneficial to me.

I'm very pleased to have gotten to know Louise Peyton, for she brought me together with Paula Stahel, whose talent and experience finally brought the manuscript to its completion.

Ann Ransford, a master English and Creative Writing teacher, once said that maybe her own "greatest contribution is just to keep the book alive." An old family friend, Ann did much more than that. She interviewed me for hours, at first in person and then later by telephone after I moved from Detroit to Tampa, Florida. She used to say that we would surely get "ring around the ear." I owe her a lot of thanks for other interviews, editing and re-writing.

Speaking of old friends, there is nothing quite as good. I owe a very special thanks to Dave Tenniswood. In addition to giving me good critical feedback—which is hard to get—on an early manuscript, when the book was on verge of incompletion, Dave intervened in a way that only Dave could. And the book got finished.

A teacher at the Michigan School for the Blind, Lucy Karner, played an important role in Stevie's and my lives. Lucy was Stevie's sixth grade teacher on the campus and was appointed to be an advisor to me during all the years leading up to Stevie earning his high school diploma. Lucy was the one I could always go to for advice or help, and always kept the rest of the school staff informed about Stevie's instruction when we were on the road. She was exceptionally helpful in keeping things running smoothly when we were in attendance at the school. A true friendship came out of our years working together and we spent many happy hours reminiscing during the development of this manuscript. She passed on a few years ago and is dearly missed by me and, I'm sure, by all of her former students.

Everyone knows about Berry Gordy, Jr., and his uncanny star-making abilities. But few people know about Dr. Robert Thompson. Dr. "T," as he was called by the students, was the superintendent of the Michigan School for the Blind. It was he who understood the need to create a unique educational experience that allowed Stevie Wonder to take advantage of his remarkable talent and unequaled professional opportunity. Dr. Thompson agreed to arrange for Stevie's education while Motown Record Company handled his career. Dr. T brought Stevie and me together, completing the team which Esther Edwards says was preordained. What Dr. Thompson was able to accomplish with his great wisdom and foresight benefited everyone on the planet. He was generous enough to share an entire day reminiscing at his retirement home in Sand Lake, Michigan, and loaned me his complete Stevie Wonder library, which he'd collected over the decades.

Several of the people I've mentioned here are no longer living. But the fruit of their labor allowed a genius to flourish. One who's constantly increasing talent and humanitarian touch continue to blossom and enrich the world with wonder—Stevie Wonder.

Chapters

The Twelve-Year-Old Who?

"We were able to find the right young man, and that man turned out to be Ted Hull. That, to me, was the most important thing that happened in Steve's career. That was the basis for everything that Stevie has become."
— *Esther Gordy Edwards*

"Mr. Hull, I think this is fate. It's as if this were divinely guided for a reason! We need a tutor to travel with Little Stevie Wonder and you're going to be perfect!"

The woman speaking to me on the phone said she was Esther Gordy Edwards, vice president of Motown Records. I got the call in September 1963. Not surprisingly, I'd never heard of her. But I'd also never heard of this "Little Stevie Wonder."

Hanging up, I turned to my long-time friend, former college roommate and now my boss, Don Cardinal. "Have you ever heard of some kid named Stevie Wonder?"

"Are you kidding?" Don looked at me in disbelief. "You're the guy with the song writing contract and you don't know the number one song in the country? *Fingertips* is all over the radio. That's Little Stevie Wonder. And he's blind."

A few days later, Esther called me again. "Stevie's doing a press conference tomorrow at one o'clock at the Graystone Ballroom. It would be a good time for you to meet him if you can be there. And we can introduce you to the press as his new tutor."

The press conference marked an unprecedented musical achievement and a significant event for Motown. Little Stevie Wonder's introduction to the Detroit media was to announce that *Fingertips Part 2* and its album, *The Twelve-Year-Old Genius*, had topped the charts. For the first time ever in recording history, one artist had both the No. 1 single and the No. 1 album in the nation.

When the media hubbub died down a little, Stevie's chaperone took his arm and led him to me. Finally able to see him, I was surprised at how young this skinny little kid seemed. Standing barely as high as my shoulder, he looked more like a happy-go-lucky nine-year-old ready to go play than a teenage singing star.

"Hello." He smiled and reached out to shake my hand. "Are you blind, too?"

* * *

As I adjusted my seat belt on the May flight from Tampa to Detroit, I remembered that meeting. In a few hours, I'd be home for the alumni reunion at the Motown Museum's grand opening. But for me, this was more than a journey of a few hours. My thoughts were carrying me back more than thirty years.

Every passenger flying with me knew Motown's music. And every single one of them knew the name Stevie Wonder. But there was something they didn't know—how I'd played a role in shaping his life. Not as a musician or a backup singer, but as his teacher and a vital member of the team who'd made his career possible. Thinking proudly of all he'd achieved over the years since we'd parted, I slipped back in a reverie to the first day I ever heard of "Little Stevie Wonder."

When Esther Gordy Edwards first phoned me, I was program director at Penrickton Center for Blind Children, a private school near Detroit, and I'd had the job for all of about two weeks.

Her voice bubbled with enthusiasm. "From what I understand about you from Dr. Thompson, you're going to be just perfect."

I had no idea who this woman was or who or what she was talking about. Only two of the things she mentioned made sense to me. Dr. Thompson, a man I knew well and respected greatly, headed the Michigan School for the Blind in Lansing. And I certainly knew of

Motown. To me it meant the Temptations, the Four Tops, Smokey Robinson and the Miracles, Martha and the Vandellas. But I'd never heard of this "Little Stevie Wonder" person she talked about.

Not wanting to sound as ignorant as I felt, I accepted her offer to meet over lunch the next day. Don didn't even hesitate about giving me time off the next day.

Mrs. Edwards had suggested we get together at Topinkas, a popular Detroit restaurant known for its high-end business lunches and the stars who dined after performing across the street at the Fisher Theater. When we met, she immediately made me feel at ease. She was a beautiful, well dressed businesswoman and obviously comfortable in her role at Motown, which had recently begun its incredible impact on the rock music industry.

Esther personal and professional poise impressed me. I think my own confidence impressed her, too. Certainly, it was exciting to have Motown want to hire me, but my life didn't hinge on whether or not that happened. I had a good job and knew I had a bright future. Yet, I was so sure of success coming my way that I wasn't surprised this was happening to me.

She told me how her brother Berry Gordy had started the company four years earlier. She'd become his vice president the previous year, leaving her job as an aide to Michigan's Governor John Swainson. Not long after, Berry had signed "Little Stevie Wonder" to a Motown contract.

As she talked, I realized the entrepreneurial spirit that ran through her family. Her father, Pop Gordy, owned a successful construction business and had provided his children a comfortable middle class life, but all were taught to be hard workers. Both he and Mrs. Gordy fostered a deep commitment to family loyalty, education and political involvement.

Esther explained that Stevie had turned thirteen just three months earlier. He was a hot young talent who'd released a couple of singles and three albums. *Tribute to Uncle Ray*, meaning Ray Charles, and *The Jazz Soul of Little Stevie Wonder* had both been well received. But it was *Fingertips Part 2*, recorded live at Chicago's Regal Theater, that rocketed him onto the charts. Primarily an instrumental with improvised words, *Fingertips* took off like gangbusters on his third album, *The Twelve-Year-Old Genius*. Now both the single and the album were hits.

As I listened to the story of the rapid success coming this child's way, my first thought was that it must be overwhelming for him. "It sounds like you need someone who can help him get over shyness about being in the limelight," I said.

"Oh, no!" Esther laughed. "That's not the problem at all. He's way beyond that. In fact, being in the limelight is what he does best."

The problem, she explained, was his education. Administrators at Fitzgerald Elementary School, where Stevie had just started sixth grade, were unhappy. Not that good a student to begin with, he was missing far too many days at school, hanging out at Motown, and his work was slipping badly.

Esther and Berry Gordy recognized Stevie's talent, but worried about his education. They knew fame could be fleeting. They also realized his talent couldn't be capitalized upon if school kept him from recording sessions or performances. His budding future was in jeopardy.

Genuinely concerned about all the performers, she knew Motown could use them, make money from them and then drop them when their popularity faded. She didn't want that to happen to anyone, but felt special responsibility for Stevie because of his age. Education was important to her personally, and she knew this young, blind, black child was likely to drop out of school as soon as it was legal, especially if it meant a chance to be a music star.

"We've been trying to get Stevie into a private school," Esther said, "because the public school is giving us so much trouble. They just don't like the idea of him being a recording artist."

As a teacher, I recognized the bind they were all in. Understandably, school administrators worried this blind youngster might be exploited. Plus, most adults then abhorred rock 'n' roll, considering it, at best, ungodly noise or, at worst, the work of the devil.

But that was beside the point. What mattered was the school held all the cards. The administrators were on Stevie's mother's case about his excessive absences. If he continued to skip classes, both he and his mother faced serious repercussions under Michigan's strict truancy laws.

Stevie preferred spending his time at the Hitsville studio, staying up late practicing and being with the other musicians. As a bright kid, I figured he was probably pretty good at manipulating his mother, Lula Mae, into believing he didn't feel well enough to go to class, although he'd be just fine by the time school was out and he could head over to Motown. I knew his mother must be in a difficult position, too, hoping that her son's talent might lift the family from its life of poverty.

During our meal, Esther told me how the idea of finding Stevie a tutor had come about, and how this led to me. Earlier in the year, the Motown Revue was booked to perform in Louisville, Kentucky. The promoter called Esther to specifically ask that Little Stevie Wonder would be in the Revue. She'd had to tell him no—Stevie couldn't afford to miss school.

This man really wanted Stevie to appear, and took it as a personal challenge to make it happen. He called Esther back a few days later to say he'd solved the problem. He knew a wonderful tutor, a kindly Southern woman named Helen Traub. A widow of about sixty, she was a retired teacher for the blind and multiple handicapped. He gave Esther her phone number.

Esther liked the idea and Mrs. Traub was soon in Detroit to meet Stevie. "They just hit it off real well," Esther said. "They hugged each other and Stevie showed her all around and they went on their way."

Mrs. Traub accompanied Stevie on the trip to Kentucky. After they returned, she told Esther that Stevie was a wonderful young boy and that she'd gladly continue as his tutor. But, she said, Stevie needed a young man to be with him, a genteel reference to the arrangements of traveling and sleeping. Even though Stevie was still a cute kid who could be tucked into hotel rooms with Mrs. Traub, the time was fast approaching when he need a man's guidance.

Mrs. Traub then made a suggestion. Knowing Stevie was qualified to attend the Michigan School for the Blind, she offered to contact the school superintendent, Dr. Thompson, for Motown.

Dr. Thompson agreed the school could gear Stevie's education around his career, allowing him to complete class work while on tour.

"'I know a young man who just graduated from Michigan State,'" Esther said he told her. "'He's worked his way around the world twice. He's partially sighted. He's a good dresser. He loves music and he's single,'" Dr. Thompson had added, and gave her my phone number. "If you hire him, we'll be the channel through which Stevie's credits will be recorded and his diploma eventually awarded."

"So, if you'll become Stevie's tutor," Esther explained, "you'll be the link between Motown and the school and between Stevie and the school."

My sole job, she said, would be to teach, ensuring Stevie met all the requirements of the Michigan School for the Blind. I would accompany him there as well as be his private tutor in Detroit and on occasional road trips. Others would take care of such things as the road management, his laundry, wardrobe and so on, she promised.

Little did either of us know, then, that Stevie's rise to fame would keep us on the road seventy-five to eighty percent of the year and that all the duties would fall to me.

As I listened and thought about her offer, I recalled her first words on the phone: "It's like this was divinely guided." Now, I felt the same way. Twenty-five and single, I had no major responsibilities tying me down. After about thirty seconds of soul searching, I jumped at the chance.

The only sticking point was money. Motown wanted to pay no more than I was earning as a special education teacher. My teacher's salary of fifty-two hundred dollars was fine for nine months of work, I said, but if I was going to teach year round, I wanted more.

Esther had a sharp mind for numbers and was a strong negotiator. "Remember, you'll be traveling the world and Motown will pay the way," she countered. "That's an advantage few people have and worth a considerable sum of money."

What she didn't know was that travel was no selling point for me. I'd spent the summer hitchhiking across Europe from London to Cairo. The summer before, I'd hitchhiked across country, traveled to Hawaii, and then hitchhiked back to Michigan. Frankly, I'd had enough of living on the road for a while.

Still, the opportunity was too good to pass up. I told her I was confident I could do the job, if we could agree on the pay.

Esther sighed. "I don't know if we can afford it. But I'll talk to Berry."

Two days later, she called. "Okay. We'll meet your salary request. We'll pay you the eight thousand dollars a year."

"Fine." Eight thousand dollars a year was darned good teaching salary. "And I want a contract."

"What do you mean, a contract?"

"I'll start working as soon as you want me to," I said, "but I want this in writing."

"Oh, all right," Esther conceded. "Now, are there any other demands or can we just get to work?"

"Stevie's doing a press conference tomorrow at one o'clock at the Graystone Ballroom," she continued. "It would be a good time for you to meet him, if you can be there. And we can introduce you to the press as his new tutor."

Working for my buddy Don was a big advantage, and he didn't hassle me for quitting my job with only twenty-four hours notice.

The next afternoon I caught a bus to the Hitsville USA office on West Grand Boulevard, then rode with Esther to the Graystone. The ballroom is gone now and even in the '60s was mostly idle unless Motown was using it. But during the '20s, '30s and '40s, it was where the famous Big Bands performed at dances for both blacks and whites.

At the Graystone, Esther turned me over to Ardena Johnston, the personal manager chaperoning Stevie that day, then left to greet the dozens of reporters on hand. When Ardena introduced Stevie to me, I was surprised at his first question: "Are you blind, too?"

I knew how important my answer would be.

"Yes," I said. "I'm not totally blind, but I am legally blind."

His smile grew wider. I could tell he was relieved, knowing my own visual impairment meant I understood his world and his life. Ardena quickly whisked Stevie away on other business, but I knew in those few minutes a bond had been created between us.

After the press conference, Esther took me back to Hitsville to show me around and introduce me to her associates. The Motown offices were in an old house, with equipment crammed everywhere. The largest area was ringed by desks and crowded with people busy over stacks of paperwork—preparing and mailing artist bios, doing promotions, finalizing contracts, setting up sessions and scheduling shows.

In the center of this activity stood a tiny office with windows all the way around, an exact replica of the foremen's offices on the Detroit automotive factory floors. Inside sat newly hired general manager Taylor Cox.

Taylor was an outgoing, energetic fellow. "If you've got any extra time, we sure could use you around here," he said enthusiastically, indicating the bustle and paperwork surrounding him.

At that moment, I had plenty of time. Even though I was already on the payroll, I was doing absolutely nothing. I responded politely but noncommittally, realizing Taylor had no understanding of my handicap. To most people, I don't appear to be visually impaired because I see well enough to travel without a white cane or guide dog. But I knew I couldn't see well enough to handle all the reading and writing required in Taylor's department without looking like a complete fool.

The next morning, Ardena Johnston took me out to meet Stevie's mother. Ardena was a gorgeous woman in her fifties with lots of sex appeal, yet she had a motherly way about her. Like nearly everyone in those early days of Motown who wasn't a Gordy relative, she was a long-time family friend. Before joining the company she'd been a social worker, experience that was a real plus in working with Stevie and his family.

Lula Hardaway and her four children lived in a rough section of west Detroit's inner city. As we walked up the three front steps to the run-down, one-story house, I stepped cautiously to avoid gaps where boards were missing in the porch floor. A huge hole gaped in the middle of the screen door. I wasn't sure whether it was due to the ghetto conditions or Stevie. I knew from experience that blind kids could be hard on screens.

A pretty young woman not much older than I opened the door and invited us in. The living room was dim and dilapidated, with worn furniture. Still, the surroundings were clean and neatly kept, a testament to Lula's standards and character.

Her voice was uneasy, though, and I sensed embarrassment, worry and distrust. I wasn't surprised. Here she was, expected to allow some unknown white guy to virtually take over her son's life. I knew with time and hard work, I might earn her trust. For now, it was enough to know that Stevie accepted me. He was still young enough to fully trust the people who had chosen me to be his teacher.

What surprised me was the tension I sensed in Lula toward Ardena, who was so dedicated to Stevie's well being. Only later would I realize this was Lula's attitude toward all the women at Motown: "Don't you try to impress *me*, honey! I know what *you* want and I *got* what you want! You be nice to me or you don't get Stevie!"

But I gave Lula credit. She knew she could put an end to Stevie's career with Motown at any time. She came close occasionally. She was a poor, uneducated young black mother with a blind son and three other kids. Suddenly, the world had begun exploding around her and her family. People were telling her, "Stevie's going to be a star. He's going to be rich." Lula hadn't been able to trust many people in her life and she sure wasn't about to trust these well dressed, well educated people from Motown.

Lula did explode periodically. "He ain't goin' to Motown no more!" she'd yell. "He was over there till two o'clock the other night. I ain't lettin' him go no more!"

After a day or two, Clarence Paul—a really good producer and quite successful song writer for Motown, would drop by. He'd sit at the family's hand-me-down piano and teach Stevie a new song. He'd cajole and argue and sweet-talk Lula. Soon, Stevie would be back in the studio.

Clarence had come up the hard way, like Lula. They spoke the same language. It was like my working with people who are blind— they trust me because of my own blindness. I don't think Berry Gordy ever realized how much Clarence Paul did to keep Stevie at Motown.

I didn't know all those things then. Nor did I know, either, that I'd spend every day of the next seven years with this talented youngster as he grew to maturity. All I knew was I was real glad to get away from Lula's tension and get started on Stevie's education.

Travelin' Man

"This is a young man who can teach Stevie many things."
— *Dr. Robert H. Thompson*

Without knowing it, I'd been preparing all my life for a job with Stevie Wonder .

At our first meeting, when Stevie asked me if I was blind, I knew how important my own visual impairment was to him. By this time, he'd met Ray Charles, but he'd never known an educated, professional adult who was blind. I'd have day to day impact on his life. From the start that made me a strong role model.

Stevie is totally blind. In 1950, when he was born, it was standard procedure to pump extra oxygen into the incubators of babies who, like Stevie, were born prematurely. The practice was necessary to the infant's underdeveloped lungs. What wasn't known then was that it led to a devastating side-effect. The extra oxygen caused blood vessels in unprotected eyes to rupture, allowing fibrous tissue to develop behind the eye and detach the retinas. The condition is called retrolental fibroplasia, or retinopathy of prematurity. Once doctors understood the cause, the practice was altered to protect the babies' eyes, but not until thousands, like Stevie, were permanently blinded.

I, on the other hand, was born with only some sight. I remember having a little light perception in my right eye when I was very young. The measurable vision in my left eye is 20/200, which is considered "legal blindness." That means I have to be twenty feet from something that people with normal, 20/20 vision can see from two hundred feet away.

Adding to the problem was that my eyes were crossed. To see something ahead of me, I had to turn my head and view it from the right or the left. Finally, when I was twenty, my eye muscles were linked surgically, allowing them to focus correctly. Having eyes that looked like they worked properly was a boon to my self-esteem, but now my right eye, which had been totally blind for years, experienced much greater muscle strain. Drinking just one beer would make that eye blood red, while the other wasn't even affected. That was almost embarrassing as being cross-eyed, and the muscle strain was uncomfortable. Eventually, my right eye was removed and replaced by a false one.

Sometimes it's hard for people with normal vision to recognize my limitations. I carry no white cane as a signal of my legal blindness. I've developed such good adaptive skills that I don't appear to have a problem until I get my nose right on top of something or walk into an obstacle. When this happens, people tend to think I'm intoxicated.

What I *can* see is hard to explain, because I don't know how most others see. People who've had vision and lose it undergo a process of adjustment to their handicap. They know what "normal" was. Neither Stevie nor I had to cope with the loss of sight. Our lives, to us, are normal.

What takes a sighted person an hour to read will take me twice as long, with the material held less than an inch from my eye. On the other hand, I can see into the distance. I can see the horizon, but only twenty percent of what someone with normal vision sees. I can see colors. I can see a car coming, because it's big and that's all I need to see to get out of the way. I can't drive a car, but I do ride a bicycle—cautiously.

Transportation is probably the biggest frustration for people who are legally or totally blind. I must walk, ride my bike, rely on city buses or expensive cabs. Friends and relatives often provide rides but those trips are made when they're ready, which isn't always convenient for me. When it comes to mobility, there's a lot of waiting and dependence caused by blindness. But I enjoy freedom and independence when I'm traveling on my own.

In our auto-driven society, getting around can be an inconvenience for the blind, just as it is for anyone without a car. Stevie's celebrity status affords him a chauffeur, a perk few people—sighted or blind—enjoy. But even totally blind people maintain their control and independence with mobility skills. Working with a trained dog guide or a white cane, people who are blind get to work, take their kids to the school bus stop, shop, go visiting, and do all the millions of little things sighted people do every day.

And part of independence, especially for kids, comes from experimenting. One night in Brooklyn, when Stevie was fifteen, I waited backstage for him to arrive before a show. He was with our chauffeur Gene Shelby, Clarence Paul and our drummer "Pistol" Allen. They were late, and I didn't like it. But the minute the four of them arrived, I sensed in their quiet moods that something unusual was up.

"What happened?" My gut feeling told me I wasn't going to like the answer.

There was silence for a moment, then Gene sheepishly admitted, "Stevie just wrecked the car."

"What?" I yelped.

"We were coming back from supper. I thought Stevie could drive a little way down the street if I told him how to steer and which way to turn. It worked."

He paused. "Until he got a heavy foot and ran into a parked car."

A teenage boy who'd seen the accident recognized Stevie getting out from behind the wheel. The boy started hollering, "What you doing? What you doing driving? You can't see!"

Never one to pass up the opportunity for a prank, Stevie turned his head this way and that. "What you say? I can't see? I didn't know that!"

The car's owner was outside by then and didn't find Stevie's joke funny. Luckily, the damage was minor. Clarence and Gene paid the man on the spot and gave him two tickets to the show.

The owner was placated. I wasn't, but I couldn't say anything. Not only because I was speechless with anger, but because I'd been just as stupid when I thought I could drive. All I could do was breathe a sigh of relief that neither Stevie's nor anyone else was injured.

I understood Stevie's wanting to experience being behind the wheel. I just kept my mouth shut about my own experiences.

For a few months between attending the Michigan School for the Blind and entering Michigan State University, I'd lived in Grand Rapids. I mentioned to my brother-in-law, Jim Starke, one day, that I'd found a Cushman Eagle motor-scooter to get around on, and wanted a driver's license. Jim, being a helpful and considerate guy, went down to the driver's license bureau. In those days, photos weren't required, so, using my name and my description, he took the test. Voila—I was legally licensed, and still legally blind.

Driving the motor-scooter wasn't much more dangerous than riding a bike, I thought, and soon decided I was quite capable of driving a car. I still have occasional nightmares about the close calls I had behind the wheel. One time, I backed into a car. Another time, I nearly ran flat out into a semi stopped on the highway. Only at the last second did I see it and swerve, barely missing it and disaster.

At that time, I sincerely believed a car was necessary for my social life, but occasionally it only caused more trouble. There was a time I got lost on my way to pick up my girlfriend at her new apartment in Lansing. At least twice I'd had to get out and climb on the front bumper to read the street signs, praying nobody would notice. By the time I reached her place, I was an hour and a half late. My date was livid. I was so embarrassed that I never admitted the truth about why I hadn't been on time.

Only once did I come close to trouble with the police. And by then, I didn't have a license anymore. I'd been caught and turned in by my counselor from the Division of Blind Services. I had mailed in my license but that didn't stop me from driving. A few months later, taking a date home, I missed her street. When I pulled behind a parked car to make a U-turn, flashing red lights erupted around us. In seconds, a police officer was at my window, demanding my license.

Well, I didn't have one and I was too scared to say so. The next thing I knew, I was being informed that the car I'd pulled behind was under stake out. Suddenly, I was under suspicion of coming to get a stolen vehicle. Now I really was nervous.

I certainly didn't help the situation by lying to the officers. I told them my license had expired so I hadn't bothered to carry it. I sat in the back of the squad car, shivering in fear while the police ran a check on me. My relief was overwhelming when the report finally came back with nothing more than confirmation of my expired license. The police wrote me a ticket and we went on our way. But I still didn't wise up. The next day, I actually drove down to the justice of the peace's office and paid my five dollar penalty. And kept right on driving.

I'll never understand why my mother and my stepfather allowed me to do something so stupid. Eventually I matured to the point where I realized I had a lot to lose if anything happened. I guess my adolescent desire for independence was greater than my common sense, so I knew I couldn't be too hard on Stevie.

Flying brought another sense of freedom. For a few years, my friend Steve Karney and I owned a Cessna 140A. I loved being up in that two-seater. While I couldn't pilot solo, I was proud to be the best non-licensed, legally blind co-pilot in the state of Michigan. Maybe in the entire United States.

I took Stevie to the airport one morning just to let him start the engine and feel the power. Another time, when we rented a twin engine plane to take us to a show in South Carolina, I talked the pilot into letting Stevie sit in the co-pilot's seat. With a light touch on the controls, he felt what it was like to fly.

Those who aren't afraid will try new things, and both Stevie and I do many more things than others with our limitations. He enjoyed riding a bike when there was nothing to run into. At the School for the Blind, roller skating in the gym was a regular recreation. Music played through speakers in the corners of the room cued Stevie and the other kids to turn as it grew louder when the neared the speakers.

He also wrestled. He wasn't on the school's team because we were gone too much, but I think he would have been a strong competitor. He loved catching me when I least expected it, trying to throw me. Fortunately, I'd been a good wrestler myself, and in all our years together, he was never able to pin me.

Giving him the opportunity for physical activity, both to burn off energy and to keep him in shape, was difficult since we spent so much time traveling or sitting backstage. Then, in 1964, the Royal Canadian

Air Force released a book about their fitness program based on isometric exercise, where muscle tone is achieved by setting one muscle against another or a fixed object. It wasn't the same as running, jumping, wrestling and the other activities the kids had at school, but it was an ideal solution to our dilemma on the road.

The rough-and-tumble fun enjoyed by kids with normal vision enjoy is available only in limited ways to blind children. It was even more so for Stevie, because he spent so much time with adults and on the road. But he and I worked under the attitude that if you can't do something about a situation, find a way to work around it.

I passed that philosophy of adaptability on to Stevie, and I credit my mother for instilling it in me. After I was grown and working with the disabled, I realized she was not a typical mother of a handicapped child. And neither was Stevie's mother. We were both raised in large families with dominant mothers who pushed their children while still protecting them. It was a reason Stevie and I meshed easily, because our mothers hadn't been afraid to let us do things on our own.

Kids always think parents are too restrictive at times, but parents of handicapped children especially have to guard against being overly protective. A lot of parents, for example, would have kept me off a bicycle because I might get hurt. Not my mom—she bought me one. She never once said "You can't do this because you're blind." She had me going to downtown Chattanooga on the bus, paying family bills and running errands by the time I was in second grade. Her confidence allowed me to find out what I could do on my own.

Stevie was also doing things independently in Detroit at an early age. I'm sure he probably scared his mother half to death many a time. But allowing him such freedom was one of the healthiest things Lula could do for her son. Even though Stevie was a black kid, totally blind, living in a big city ghetto culture, and I'm white, legally blind, and was raised in the South, our mothers gave us the same confidence to tackle the world.

I'd been born outside of Jamestown, Tennessee, a small town near the Cumberland Gap. This beautiful, mountainous area was featured in the Gary Cooper movie *Sergeant York*, and the World War I hero still lived nearby when I was born in 1937. Another famous name in the area was a distant relative—Cordell Hull, Secretary of State under President Franklin D. Roosevelt when Pearl Harbor was attacked. When he received the Nobel Peace Prize in 1945, the entire family felt an enormous sense of pride.

Our family had a long history in the mountains, and included a wide variety of characters from moonshiners, such as Cordell's dad, to educated entrepreneurs like my grandfather, who owned sawmills.

The first school I attended was a two-teacher, one-room school in Armathwaite, Tennessee. First, second, third and fourth grades were on one side of a curtain and fifth, sixth, seventh and eighth grades were on the other side, with two teachers and a helper. I'd sit all day with nothing to do and was rarely noticed. Except once. After eating an apple at my desk, I decided to toss it out the open window near me. But the window wasn't open—until it broke. That's the only time I remember getting any attention.

At six, I was sent off to Junior Military Academy in Cookeville, Tennessee. Every new boy had to run a gauntlet, being pushed, paddled and beaten by the other. The first morning, my two roommates got into a fight—not just horsing around but really going at each other. The "sergeant," a boy about fifteen, came in and used a buggy whip on all three of us. It didn't matter that I wasn't fighting. I hadn't even been at the school twelve hours and had already been beaten up twice. It was a rude awakening.

I was so homesick that year. I never told my mother about those incidents or any of the other horrifying things I witnessed. Like the time I watched the Major, the school headmaster, literally drag a teenage boy across campus and bash his head against a door jamb three times, then throw him into the office and paddle the daylights out of him. Or the day an older boy out in the campus woods was shot, probably by a hunter. The bullet passed through his right arm and on through his body. He was brought in and laid on the porch. Screaming in pain, he couldn't even close his mouth because of all the vomit and blood pouring out. Experiences like that strongly fostered my independence.

Experiences like that strongly fostered my independence. My mother never knew any of this to her dying day, nor why, after that year, I didn't seem to need her very much anymore.

My father, an intelligent but poorly educated man, had a lot of big dreams that drove him to find a better life away from the Tennessee mountains. I went to school all around the country. Indiantown, Florida. Muncie, Indiana. The Clara Carpenter School in Chattanooga; there, Mrs. Bredin was my first, trained special education teacher. Because she knew how to teach me, I finally began to learn. And the School for the Blind in Nashville.

Eventually, my father's restlessness led the family west, to San Diego. By then, I was thirteen and in sixth grade, extremely verbal, and could hardly spell my own name. I was put into a class full of rough boys whose self-esteem problems were compounded by handicaps. Their unruliness left the sensitive, well trained teacher in tears by the end of nearly every day. She was excited to have me as a student because I was related to Cordell Hull. Her pride in me felt good, but also made me worry I could never live up to her expectations.

Soon we moved again, this time to Portland, Oregon. There, my junior high teacher put no pressure on me. She didn't teach me much of anything, either, but did love me dearly. I couldn't see the blackboard or read the textbooks, so I'd sit in the back of the room with my talking books while the other kids read aloud. I'd often just fall asleep. The teacher would shush the other kids, telling them, "Don't make a lot of noise, we don't want to wake up Ted." Once a week a special education teacher came to work with me, which only made me feel more self-consciousness.

My increasing diffidence, the constant moving and being in classrooms where the teachers didn't know what to do with me, led to problems. Like Stevie, I started skipping school. I fell in with a bad crowd because they made me feel accepted. None of them owned a car, but they'd invite me to go joy-riding—and I always made darned sure to not ask how they'd gotten the wheels. That let me pretend I didn't know the cars were stolen.

After attending several high schools in Portland, I was sent to live with my aunt in Battle Creek, Michigan, twice inside of two years. I lived with one of my sisters in San Francisco and went to school near Candlestick Park for several months. I remember the School for the Blind in Salem, Oregon, and the one in Worthington, Ohio, where I finally spent a complete year in the same school.

My parents had split up by this time and I was living with my father. Our parents being divorced was another thing Stevie and I would have in common. Eventually I returned to Michigan and spent my senior year at the School for the Blind. Dr. Thompson came on the scene that same year.

I'd attended eighteen different schools before college. Such a disruptive education could have caused me to give up on school all together. Instead, it was excellent preparation for the situations I encountered teaching Stevie on the road, and gave me the confidence to tackle anything that came my way. I think my ability to roll with the punches helped give Stevie the ability to discover that strength in himself.

But all the moving about had left me without a solid understanding of what elementary education was all about. This worried me, and preparing Stevie's lessons was a daily struggle. I'd be up at six a.m. to cram for the next four hours, making sure I was ready to teach him. I doubt I'd ever have become as good as Lucy Karner, Stevie's sixth grade teacher at the School for the Blind. By teaching the same grade every year in one place, she had the advantage of honing her skills and becoming an outstanding teacher. On the other hand, I could pull things together and get the job done under all sorts of circumstances. And I offered Stevie many other things a classroom couldn't, such as first-hand lessons in social studies, real life experiences in the world, and the individual support he needed to succeed with his talent.

* * *

After attending the Michigan School for the Blind for my senior year, I was still one credit shy of graduation. Moving again, to Grand Rapids, I completed that high school credit and took some college prep courses at Aquinas College before moving once more, this time to live with my mother and stepfather in Lansing. One day, my mother said, "Classes start next week at Michigan State. You'd better get registered."

I still wasn't ready for college, but that didn't stop me. Or my mother, who lobbied for the university to give me a chance. I'd never written a book report, compiled an outline or studied fractions. I couldn't even read the entrance exams. But at that time, getting into college was different than today. I was accepted on probation.

It was in college that I learned to play guitar and, with my friend Tony Juliano, began to write songs. Although we had no professional success, we did land a song writing contract with ABCO Publishing in Nashville. Every artist seemed to have his own publishing company then and things were so informal. Anyone could drop by, have his music heard and, just by showing talent, walk out with a contract.

I often had trouble studying because I was more interested in writing lyrics, but college life was also free and easy. I never expected I'd earn a living at music. It was just a lot of fun, and a lot easier than struggling through my courses.

It helped to know several other students who'd also attended the School for the Blind. We had a reading room in the Michigan State University library where Tower Guards, girls with B-plus averages, volunteered as readers. An added benefit was that some of the Tower Guards were knockouts and enriched my social life immensely. Without all the girls' help, I more than likely would have failed. The only way I could study was to have every single textbook read to me. And most of my exams, as well.

But once I settled on a major, both my interest in classes and my grades began to improve. My plan to study restaurant management changed when I realized my experiences as a visually impaired student gave me a unique understanding of special education and rehabilitation. Also, my mother believed teaching to be the world's most important career. I graduated with a degree in special education for the visually impaired in 1962.

My first job was teaching mentally retarded children in Dansville, Michigan, hometown of the Studebaker. Although not trained to work with the mentally handicapped, I made the best of it for the semester. After substitute teaching the visually impaired in Dearborn, I was hired by Penrickton, the school for multiple handicapped blind children, where Esther Gordy Edwards found me.

An advantage of teaching was having summers off. Wanting to see how the rest of the world lived before settling down, I'd spent the previous summers traveling, first across the USA, then through Europe twice—first on a Euro-Rail pass, and then hitchhiking from London to Cairo and back on less than five dollars a day. I took a train over the Balkan Mountains in Yugoslavia and through parts of Greece where the temperature was one hundred and ten degrees. I booked deck passage, the cheapest thing I could get, to cross the Aegean.

In Egypt I met an Irish fellow and we decided to go to the Suez Canal. The Egyptians and the English were at war, and we wanted to see what all the fighting was about. Getting out the map, we found a little village called Suez. Figuring this was where the action was, off we went, only to find nothing but horse and camel dung in the streets. We were in the wrong place—totally. Our presence attracted the attention of the military police, who immediately arrested us.

We'd both heard stories about people being arrested and never seen again. Detained at headquarters and questioned for a couple of hours, the guy with me didn't help matters at all by repeatedly cursing and yelling, "I told you I'm from Ireland. What's the matter with you?" Finally, the officers were convinced we weren't spies. They told us about a truck heading to Cairo and strongly suggested we get out of town.

We were more than glad to oblige and struck a deal with the driver for a ride. But when we arrived in Cairo, he'd decided to triple his price. We refused, literally threw what money we had into the cab, and ran. He had three friends in the truck who could have easily beaten or killed us. We didn't stick around to find out which.

By the time I left Egypt, I'd run out of money. My only possession was a little transistor radio. Selling it for eleven dollars, I made it to Athens. There, I sold two pints of blood for thirteen dollars. It was all I had to get me back to Amsterdam. For the first time in my life I was hungry and couldn't do anything about it.

My hitchhiking adventures were written up in the Lansing newspaper, where Dr. Thompson read about my journeys. When Esther Gordy Edwards called him for help finding a tutor, it was one of the mental filings that led to his recommending me.

Sometimes, looking back, I'm amazed at the things I did with absolutely no fear. But the experiences taught me to think quickly, deal with whatever happened, stay strong and meet things head on. It was ideal training for all the situations I'd encounter with Motown.

Like dealing with promoters. My job as Stevie's tutor quickly expanded to making sure Stevie and Motown received fair payment for shows. While a show was going on, the promoter and I were busy adding up ticket sales and expenses before dividing the proceeds. Some of those guys could get mighty creative when it came to accounting. There were a lot of gimmicks they could use to cut our share. If Stevie was supposed to get ten percent of the box office take on top of his fee, they'd claim, "We sold 10,000 tickets" when they'd actually sold 14,000.

A promoter in South Carolina, in particular, was known for such creative accounting. The first time anyone did one of his shows, they found him to be the most charming, gracious, helpful promoter they'd ever dealt with, and couldn't understand why other performers warned them to watch out for their pay and their backs. Then they'd catch his ticket takers slipping every fifth ticket stub into a pocket instead of the counting box. Or they'd find themselves stranded after a show in some remote burg, with no transportation home.

It was people like that who proved the value of my independent travels. On those hitchhiking trips, I'd quickly learned that, as a stranger in a strange land, I had to look out for myself. Now, the strange new land I was in was the music industry, and I was responsible for Stevie and Motown as well as myself. Most of the time I felt the promoters played straight with us because I watched everything carefully, and they didn't get upset with my close scrutiny. What I hoped they didn't know was that I didn't always know what to watch them for.

On the other hand, there were some truly scrupulous folks in the business. Henry Wynn owned the popular Peacock Lounge in Atlanta. When he put on a tour, musicians clamored to be part of it. The first night I worked with him, he handed me a brown paper bag containing Stevie's pay. I sat myself down on his office floor to count it. Henry was absolutely outraged and insulted that I didn't trust him. Unfortunately, his honesty didn't extend to the IRS—Henry died in prison, serving time for income tax evasion.

* * *

The first thing I needed to do after being hired as Stevie's tutor, though, was get an understanding of the schooling he'd had so far. I met with his special education teacher at Fitzgerald Elementary School to review his work and her impression of him. He was a sixth grader, but I quickly realized he'd missed so much school that we needed to start at the fifth grade level.

Next, I headed to Lansing to meet with the staff at the School for the Blind. We developed a curriculum for Stevie, and I equipped myself for his lessons. That meant braille and print books, teachers' manuals, a talking book machine and tape recorder, a Perkins braille writer, a slate and stylus and braille paper so Stevie could improve his reading and writing skills, plus a cube board used for teaching math. I headed back to Detroit and met with the Motown staff, to explain how Stevie's schooling would work.

Before I knew it, I was back on the road, this time with a student in tow.

Someone To Turn To

"Ted was the bridge between Stevie and the school and Stevie and the company. We had no problems whatsoever because Ted was with him."

— *Esther Gordy Edwards*

Within a week of joining Motown, music director Clarence Paul, Stevie and I set out in the Motown station wagon that Gene Shelby drove for us. Over the years, Gene and Clarence became my trusted friends. On that trip, though, I clearly sensed their wariness. Until now, they'd been Stevie's protectors, responsible for many of the duties I was taking over. And I was white, to boot. To win their confidence, I knew I'd have to prove my competence.

My first opportunity came when we stopped at a roadside restaurant in Indiana. A young man shyly approached our lunch table to ask for Stevie's autograph. This was still a new and thrilling experience for Stevie. On the rare occasions he'd been asked in the past, someone else signed his name to a promotional photo or slip of paper.

As Clarence reached for his pen, I quickly pulled out mine and placed it in Stevie's hand. "Here," I said, "I'll guide your hand while you write your name."

"Oh!" Stevie's pleased smile then burst into an enormous grin. He squirmed with excitement as our hands spelled out his name across a wallet-sized photo. I knew what this seemingly simple act meant to him—the ability to take control of a little larger part of his life.

After his happy fan left, Gene, Clarence and Stevie finished their meals and went to the restroom. I followed a couple minutes later, coming up behind Clarence sputtering in disgust.

"He doesn't even know how to spell your name! At least he ought to be able to spell your name right!"

An awkward silence fell. I pretended not to have heard Clarence's remark, but I was honestly puzzled. I hadn't seen Stevie's name written down anywhere, but how could I get it wrong? It rhymed with the name I was called at home—Teddy.

As soon as I had the chance, I took a careful look at one of Stevie's record labels, and never made the mistake again! Somewhere, someone's got the only authentic, one-of-a-kind autograph from 1963, signed "Little Stevy Wonder."

* * *

We were making the overnight trip to Chicago to record Stevie's first string album. Rock was still such an emerging genre that artists were expected to do two things to build their careers. One was to record an album backed by a string orchestra, to demonstrate their ability with standard songs. The second was to do a Country/Western album, which Stevie never did. But over the years I influenced his interest in country music and Clarence wrote arrangements of two songs that always pleased Stevie's audiences: Willie Nelson's *Funny How Time Slips Away*, and *Walkin' The Floor Over You*, an Ernest Tubb hit from the 1950s.

After checking into a hotel, we headed to a recording studio where the Chicago Symphony Orchestra's twenty-eight-piece string section was waiting. Also there was someone we hadn't expected—Barbara Lewis, who had a hit then with *Hello Stranger* on the Atlantic Records label.

Barbara and I sat in a small observation room, separated by a glass wall from the recording area where Clarence and Stevie worked. She was friendly but just watched quietly as everyone bustled about. The studio had been booked for only a three-hour session and I realized quickly that this was serious work where every second was money, not a friendly jam. While Barbara concentrated on watching how this young blind boy worked, I concentrated on the blindisms I was noticing in Stevie.

"Blindisms" are repetitive physical mannerisms often developed unconsciously by people who are blind. At the piano, Ray Charles rocks his upper body side-to-side. Stevie's main blindism was even more pronounced—he rotated his whole upper body in a wide circle. It was a habit I'd already noticed, but as the recording session progressed, I realized this action became even more exaggerated when he felt under pressure. We'd have to work on this, I thought, because it would distract audiences. Soon, we set up signals, such as a snap of my fingers, to remind him of this blindism. He didn't really get it under control until he became interested in girls a few years later. Now, Stevie's blindism is minor, but it's an identifying trait that actor Eddie Murphy uses so successfully in an outstanding imitation of his friend—shoulders back, face lifted, head bobbing side to side as he sings.

I also knew audiences would automatically give Stevie a certain amount of applause just because he was blind. Determined to keep him from capitalizing on this pity factor, I watched carefully to find ways to build his personal control and independence.

The session was educational for both of us, but difficult for Stevie. The strings were beautiful and so were the songs, standards such as *With a Song In My Heart* and *Sunny Side of the Street.* Yet these weren't the types of songs he was used to performing. Compounding his anxiety was the fact that his voice had begun to change suddenly and he had trouble with the high notes. Stevie did his best, but neither he nor Clarence were really pleased with the work.

Several days later, Esther and I were using her brother's office for a meeting to tie up some loose ends of my "contract." (Barely one paragraph, it wouldn't have held up in a toilet, let alone in a court of law. Which made it an excellent agreement from Motown's position.) The office, outfitted with all sorts of playback equipment and fantastic speakers on the wall, was where Berry listened to new music. As Esther and I talked, Berry came in with one of his sons and a photographer, to take the youngster's picture seated at his dad's large desk. Esther introduced me to her brother, who was cordial but preoccupied with having his son's picture done.

Before leaving, though, Berry took a minute to listen to a few bars from the Chicago recording session. Right away it was obvious he was not at all pleased, as he mimicked Stevie's strained efforts to hit his high notes. But there wasn't anything to be done then. The session was over and the album would be released. Berry silently accepted the fact that it would do nothing for Motown or Stevie's career.

Stevie's adolescent growth definitely posed a problem. If he couldn't be counted on to hit the right notes, his career and Motown's investment in him were both at risk. No one knew how long it would take for his voice to change or how it would ultimately sound. It hadn't entered my mind till then that my job might be short-lived if Stevie lost his singing voice or if his popularity faded.

Still, that disappointing recording session ultimately proved valuable to Stevie. Years later Clarence Paul told me it was probably one of the most significant learning situations Stevie encountered in his early days. At the time, he listened mostly to rhythm and blues and rock 'n' roll. Both forms of music are very simple, usually with only three or four chords. In Chicago, the symphony orchestra exposed him to traditional melodies with sophisticated chord progressions. He and Motown didn't get a hot-selling album, but Stevie's musical genius benefited with ideas that eventually blossomed in other songs.

Everything was a learning experience for him. Unfortunately, some of the lessons were more beneficial to his character than to his creativity. Especially during the first year I worked with him.

Stevie was still building his fame that winter when he was booked for two appearances in Canada. Little Stevie Wonder was virtually unknown outside of Windsor, just across the river from Detroit, and Canadians heavily favored C&W over rock. On top of this, the promoter was inexperienced and an extremely heavy drinker. Before a show, Clarence and I watched him down an eight-ounce tumbler of straight whiskey as if it were water. At the 6,000-seat Montreal auditorium, we realized college fraternities had put more people into Volkswagens than were in the audience.

"Stevie, there are less than two dozen people out there," Clarence told him. "But these people are your fans. They bought a ticket and we're not going to shortchange them. We do the whole show."

From Montreal, we headed to the smaller town of Kitchener. For reasons I'm sure were logical to the promoter's liquor-laden mind, he had us riding in a winter parade at eight in the morning. It was so cold when we climbed into the open Cadillac convertible that we had to borrow an overcoat for Stevie—only it was so big that you could hardly find Stevie. Not that anyone was looking. Not one living soul was out to see this grand, three-car "parade." First, hardly anyone at Stevie's show, now no people on the street. Experiences like that teach performers a lot—about disappointment and being humble.

And Stevie's education was my first and foremost responsibility. Over the years it turned into an exhausting responsibility.

*   *   *

Initially, things fell into a smooth pattern when we weren't on the road. Gene Shelby would pick up Stevie in the morning and bring him to my apartment, where we'd hold classes. In the afternoon, Gene drove Stevie to the Motown studio to record.

My decision to start Stevie back at the beginning of fifth grade class work really didn't set him back. If there were things he didn't need to study, we skipped over them. I just wanted to be sure he had the basic skills he needed. Up through fifth grade, a teacher focuses on helping students learn to study independently. By sixth grade, a teacher should feel confident that the student can follow instructions such as, "Open your book and study chapter six, then write a paragraph about what you've read." In Stevie's case, that meant reading and writing braille.

I recognized quickly that if Stevie had remained in a regular classroom, at best and with a lot of effort, he might have been only an average student. What really impressed me was his desire to please me by completing all his homework. I knew it wasn't easy, with calls from the studio and all the other aspects of his growing fame.

Motown constantly created distractions. It took a few arguments on my part before the staff learned they had to make arrangements directly with me, not with Stevie or his mother.

From the start, I insisted Stevie was to lead as balanced a life as possible. I knew he had a heavy load, but I was a stickler about separating his personal and professional lives. The flexible way Motown operated worked to my disadvantage. Basically, the studio never closed. No matter what hour of the day or night, if a producer or songwriter had an idea, they'd call and say, "Let's go record this."

At first, producers or musicians tried sneaking Stevie into the studio, hoping I wouldn't find out. But when he'd arrive the next morning too tired to stay awake, I knew he'd spent half the night there. It was bad enough he wasn't getting his rest, but making things worse was that he spent so much time just hanging out with the musicians.

When they weren't working, the guys would sit out in their cars, talking and usually drinking and smoking. When I found out what Stevie was being exposed to, I laid down the law. He wasn't to be at the studio past eight o'clock, and he was forbidden from the cars, because that's where all the "action" took place. Esther and I strongly enforced the rules.

While I was fairly sure the guys weren't giving Stevie booze or pot, there were only a few people I trusted to be with him when I wasn't around. Clarence Paul, Beans Bowles and Hank Cosby were all protective of Stevie in very fatherly ways. Clarence was a real carouser, representing absolutely everything you wouldn't want a young boy exposed to, but I knew he always treated Stevie with respect and never tried to involve him in anything harmful.

To most of the Motown musicians, Stevie wasn't a peer. He was a kid, a toy. They reveled in the fact that he was a sponge for all their musical knowledge. I just had to make sure he didn't absorb more than he needed to know at such a young age.

For more than a year, I didn't have a night off on the road. Then, Gene Shelby offered to let Stevie stay overnight with him. Oh, how I relished that short break and looked forward to more! But when I knocked on Gene's hotel room door the next morning, I was in for a surprise.

"Is Stevie ready to go?" I asked.

"No, he's still in bed." Gene opened the door wider and stepped back. "Come on in."

I glanced at the form under the covers. Something wasn't right—Stevie wasn't that long when he stretched out in bed. Then I saw a second bed and immediately recognized Stevie there.

Gene had had another overnight guest—one of his many women. He didn't see anything wrong with the situation, since Stevie had his own bed. I didn't quite see it that way. Stevie was blind, but he wasn't deaf. And he was way too young and too smart to be exposed to Gene's act as a ladies' man. That was the last time I let Stevie spend the night with anyone else. It was my last break for many more months, until I felt Stevie was independent enough to stay alone is his hotel room.

Motown's scheduling of recording sessions during school hours was another problem, one that often caught unsuspecting souls in the middle. In 1965, when we had a real battle going for a while, Berry's brother Robert called and said, "They want Stevie at the studio tomorrow afternoon at two. It's very important."

"No," I said. "That's Stevie's school time. Our routine is important and I'm not going to break it. Tell them they'll have to reschedule."

"Okay," he agreed. "I'll talk to them and call you back."

Not three minutes later, the phone rang again. As soon as I answered, Robert exclaimed, "I'm beginning to feel like a Ping-Pong ball!"

"I know, Robert," I sympathized. "But if I give in this time, tomorrow it's going to be the same thing. This isn't something new. I have to put up with it all the time."

I understood the rough spot Robert was in, but I wasn't about to compromise. Yet.

As it turned out, the session was to record *I Was Made To Love Her*, and Stevie's mother was one of the credited writers. Next thing I knew, Lula was on the phone, trying to charm me into changing my mind. In a way, it was kind of funny, because I knew that when Lula called, it meant Motown had run out of arguments to use with me. And actually, I was kind of impressed because no one ever made the demand that "This is how it is and you're the one who's going to fit our schedule."

"Ted, can't he do it just this once?" she begged sweetly. "If you'll make an exception just this time, I'll make sure you get your reward."

I gave up and gave in. (But Lula Mae, I'm still waiting.)

* * *

As Stevie's tutor and companion on the road, I was with him literally twenty-four hours a day. Lessons were worked around travel and performances. My flexibility and self-discipline were tested constantly.

The amount of chaperoning Stevie required was compounded by both his blindness and his age. I had to be available for press conferences, reporters and radio DJs, who seemed to come out of the woodwork with no appointments. I had to observe and monitor their interviews with Stevie to ensure they went well and that the information was what Motown wanted fans to hear.

Performances often kept us in theaters until one or two in the morning. No matter how late we got to bed, I made sure Stevie got at least eight hours of sleep. I wasn't so well rested. No matter how late I'd come in or how tired I was, my alarm went off at six so I could prepare Stevie's lessons and keep up with our expense accounting.

Having student-taught five and sixth grades, I was familiar with those grades, which made it easier for me. But working classes around show schedules was especially difficult for both of us. Stevie'd go on as the headline act, working up a tremendous sweat, with people screaming and dancing in the aisles as he performed hard for forty-five minutes. Then he'd come back to the dressing room, change out of his stage outfit and hear me say, "Okay, we've got two hours before the next show. Let's get going on spelling and math."

It was a constant challenge to find places we could do lessons. We couldn't always work in the dressing room. At most of the traditional theaters, like New York City's Apollo, there weren't enough dressing rooms for us to have a private one. On the bill there'd probably be ten other artists, plus the band, the backstage crews and managers. Everybody used the Apollo's "dungeon," a basement area about as comfortable as its name. At other theaters, we didn't share dressing rooms with acts from outside Motown, but Gene Shelby and Clarence Paul traveled with us. They did their best to try to stay out of our way, but sometimes I'd have to take Stevie out in the hallway or find a backstage corner where we could study without interruption.

I didn't enjoy working the traditional theaters. The surrounding neighborhoods were blighted and the schedule was extremely hard on everyone. At the Apollo, for instance, we'd have three shows on Friday, starting the first one around four p.m. and not leaving until at least one o'clock the next morning, Saturday's matinee then at ten a.m., with four more shows running late into the night. While there might be two or three hours between Stevie's appearances, it wasn't enough time to leave the theater to do anything else.

The waiting was boring, at least for me. Stevie enjoyed himself when we weren't studying, because there was a constant parade of people coming through to talk or get his autograph. He had a wonderful time. I would have, too, if I'd been him.

Since Stevie was following the same curriculum as his classmates at the Michigan School for the Blind, I knew when I was expected to have certain lessons completed and could judge the best time for school work. Sometimes I'd have a feeling we wouldn't be able to do lessons at the theater because Stevie's mind would be on the upcoming show or because of problems we knew were going to exist. Times like that just weren't good for schooling. It wasn't unusual to skip classes while traveling on Friday, do shows that night, and then have class between shows on Saturday and Sunday. Often, it was the only way we could fit lessons in. Plus, on weekends, there wasn't much else to do. It helped keep Stevie's mind and hands busy on those days when other teenagers were sleeping in late and goofing off. At the same time, I'd remind him that, because of his schedule, we often didn't have school when those other teens did.

The need to get school work done did deliver one advantage. To make sure Stevie had time for lessons and the rest he needed, Motown allowed us to travel by plane to any show more than two hundred miles away. The other performers didn't have that luxury.

In a regular classroom, Stevie might have been able to get by without doing some of the work, but with me constantly by his side he didn't even try. He knew it wouldn't work. Occasionally, though, on the

Motown Revue bus he'd pretend to be asleep. Sometimes I'd pretend to believe it, because I didn't want to do the lessons then either.

It was very difficult to work on the bus so I usually kept the lessons brief. In that setting, where everyone could hear us, Stevie was self-conscious as a student and I was self-conscious as a teacher. But we simply had to get the work done and often the only time available was while traveling between shows.

We did bring a certain sophistication, I think, to the Motown bus. Tours would include the Temptations, the Miracles, the Supremes, Martha & the Vandellas, Choker Campbell and the band, and Shorty Long, who'd written *Devil With The Blue Dress On*. All these people were out to sing songs, make some money, play some poker and have some fun. Their minds weren't really on the future. It was my struggle to teach Stevie to think about his future and realize the importance of his education. I found it interesting that it also became important to the others, many of whom were high school drop-outs or hadn't been raised to value education highly.

There were people on the tours who understood what I was trying to do. I could always count on Esther and Berry Gordy, the emcee Bill "Winehead Willie" Murray, plus Clarence, Beans Bowles and Smokey Robinson. Out of forty people or so, there were always a handful who were supportive and influenced the others. When things got rowdy, I'd hear someone like Smokey or Diana Ross say, "Shush, be quiet. Ted's trying to teach Stevie," or, "Keep the bad language down. There's a youngster on the bus."

No one really objected or was resentful. The other acts and musicians valued Stevie as an important part of Motown. If he'd been required to attend a regular classroom and couldn't tour, a lot of musicians knew they'd have been out of steady work.

Exactly because Stevie wasn't confined to a school campus, the world became his classroom. Rarely does any teacher have the opportunity to combine lessons with life the way I could for Stevie. As wearisome as our travel and show schedules could be, I found time for as many field trips as possible.

43

I made a point of taking Stevie to a school for the blind when we were in foreign countries. In Paris, he sat at the table where Louis Braille had studied a hundred years before. He experienced a day in the life of blind students in Japan. And everywhere, we pursued the culture. In Japan, we went to a tea ceremony school. In England, a guard at the Tower of London opened glass cases so Stevie could handle priceless items, including Maximillian's silver armor and the armor for his horse. We toured the Rotterdam harbor on a trip to the Netherlands. We read *The Diary of Anne Frank* before visiting the attic in Amsterdam where she and her family were hidden for years. After being interviewed by the press, Stevie would turn the tables and interview the reporters for social studies assignments.

American history became more than just stories in books as we traveled our own country. Show dates in the nation's capitol allowed us to visit all the famous monuments. George Washington's legendary crossing of the Delaware River became a personal experience when I rented a canoe for the two of us, then handed Stevie a paddle. The vastness of the Atlantic Ocean became a reality at the beach in Ft. Lauderdale. Standing barefoot at the water's edge, Stevie drank in sounds of gulls and the scent of the salt water. And, unexpectedly, its taste. Seemingly out of nowhere an enormous wave roared ashore, drenching us both from head to toe and permanently ruining the stage outfit he was wearing.

Every place we visited, new obstacles had to be overcome. These presented opportunities to instill Stevie with my confidence as a person with severe visual impairment and my confidence in his abilities as a blind person. Once in a while, though, it was my own blindness that contributed to our difficulties.

At the Statue of Liberty, I accidentally brought us a unique grasp of how salmon must feel swimming upstream. Like most tourists, Stevie and I wanted to climb to the top of Lady Liberty. Making our way up the one-hundred forty-two narrow, winding steps, a steady stream of people passed us going the other direction. We often were forced to press against the wall to let them by. I thought it a bit odd that we never caught up anyone else heading in our direction. At the top, I found out why.

Stevie and I had climbed up the down staircase. I hadn't even seen the big red "Exit" sign over the door I'd led him through.

Finding public facilities in unfamiliar places also was a problem at times, and often led to some embarrassing but funny situations. On one trip through Britain, there was no bathroom on the tour bus. By the time we arrived at the auditorium in Wales, everyone was pretty uncomfortable. Dashing ahead of the others, Stevie and I darted into the darkened backstage bathroom. Finding what we thought was the urinal, we let fly. One of the Temptations came in and turned on the light. There Stevie and I stood, relieving ourselves into a bathtub.

Other experiences taught me about humility in different ways.

During the early 1960s, Hollywood was trying to cash in on rock 'n' roll. Soon, Stevie was cast to sing in *Muscle Beach Party*, starring Frankie Avalon and former Mouseketeer Annette Funicello. Like the other "rock" films being done then, the story line was unbelievably lame and most of the music was downright lousy. Stevie was forced to do some incredibly dumb numbers, including an exceptionally silly tune called *Happy Street*. Still, the chance to be in a movie was too important to be passed up.

Our first day at the studio, I was preparing to start his lessons when an older woman introduced herself. "I'll be Stevie's teacher while he's in Hollywood," she said.

"I'm Stevie's teacher," I informed her sharply.

"That may be, but I've been assigned to do the teaching while he's here." She explained patiently that California's strict laws required the state to provide a backstage teachers for all minors.

Well, that hurt my pride and ticked me off.

"Just what are your qualifications?" I demanded. "I'm a certified teacher for the blind. Are you?"

"No," she admitted.

"Then I'll take care of this," I informed her in a huff. I phoned her supervisor, to whom I pointed out that as Stevie's tutor, as a certified teacher for the blind *and* as a graduate of Michigan State University, I was fully qualified to handle his education in any state.

The man's response was rather cool. "Well, that's the way it is here in California."

"Look," I said, "he's my student. I'm certified. She isn't. And I'll do the teaching."

Now his voice turned cold. "Either you do it our way or you can take your Little Stevie Wonder back to Michigan."

Okie-dokie! So be it. I'd lost that battle, but I still wasn't about to concede the war. I went back to the other teacher.

"All right," I said. "I guess I have no choice. Here's his lesson plan. The day's first lesson is braille."

There was a long moment of confusion on her part and internal gloating on mine.

"Well, why don't we work together?" she finally suggested. "You teach him the braille and I'll teach him some of the other things."

It actually turned out to be a pleasant experience working with her. She was a nice, concerned person and I enjoyed her help once I put aside my pride.

In his own way, Stevie was learning a similar lesson. While making a movie was fun, he had to learn to live with the disappointment of having no lines and only being "used" as a singer.

But I still had one more lesson to learn, about paying attention to how others perceived Stevie.

After filming was complete, a cast party was held on the movie set. Always on the lookout for practical learning examples, I spotted a great opportunity in the party decorations.

"Stevie, they've got balloons filled with helium." I grabbed one by the string and handed it to him. "Tomorrow we'll do a science class on lighter-than-air gasses."

A few moments later I overheard someone say, "Look at that. Can you believe how immature Stevie Wonder is? He's fourteen and still plays with balloons!"

I was both embarrassed and angry, but I realized that's exactly how it appeared. From then on, I was much more careful of how people might interpret Stevie's actions.

Stevie's very public life made it especially important to me to teach him the fine points of both personal and social habits. These little niceties of life are often difficult for blind people to learn outside of a residential school setting. Besides, growing up in the South, I just assumed such lessons were part of life.

Dining at fine restaurants became an opportunity to teach proper table etiquette, such as how to handle silverware and identify where food is placed, both on the table and on the plate. When we traveled with the Motown Revues, I think I occasionally made some of the others feel awkward for having had few table manners drilled into them as children. I insisted Stevie put his napkin in his lap, use the correct fork properly, or spoon soup toward the back of the bowl. Such things simply had been ingrained in me at the family table. And, I knew, they certainly were skills that a star such as Stevie needed to know, and knew his mother would appreciate.

But I also understood every rule had its exceptions. On a trip in England, everyone on the bus was starving when we finally made a quick stop. It was one of those times to forget propriety. One of the Temptations, sitting at a nearby table, saw Stevie using his fingers to push a piece of chocolate pie and whipped cream into his mouth. "Hey, get it, Stevie!" he called out. My dirty look brought an immediate apology. Between Stevie's hunger and the few minutes we had to eat, I knew it wasn't the place to make an object lesson out of proper dining.

At thirteen, Stevie had begun experiencing a life his family could barely imagine. Stevie was always welcome to use the phone as much as he wanted, to talk to his family. He liked sharing the excitement of visiting new places and doing new things. I admired Lula for the way she handled her feelings and those of his brothers and sister. Lula never once told Stevie not to do something because of his blindness, or because others in the family couldn't do what he was doing. And she did have to counsel her other children when they became jealous of Stevie.

Lula told me once that Stevie's brother Larry would ask, "How come I can't do what he does?"

"I tried to explain to him that Stevie is good at music," she said, "and maybe not everybody is going to be good at music. Maybe you'll excel at basketball or baseball. But don't try to be like Stevie. Because Stevie can do something doesn't mean you can do it. Find what you're good at, and you'll be happy."

Lula may not have been an educated woman, but I respected her motherly wisdom greatly.

I wasn't in touch with Lula much more than any other teacher is probably in touch with a student's parents. I called her when necessary, but generally things went well. She'd call me if she was concerned about something. When a minor problem arose, I'd just take care of it, often forgetting that Lula might wonder what was going on.

But with Dr. Thompson and others at the School for the Blind, things were very different. I kept them closely informed about Stevie's progress. I filed quarterly reports and asked the company to do them also. We all knew that when a tour was over, Stevie had to be ready to fit in again at school. There'd be no famous singers and musicians, no groupies or recording sessions. It would be a break when he could just be a kid, like all the others.

No Sad Boy

"Dr. Thompson, thank you for bringing Ted Hull and me together, for you and Ted are instrumental in making this fantasy come true."

> — *Stevie Wonder*
> *June 9, 1974*

As soon as I met Stevie after his first day as a fifth grader at the Michigan School for the Blind, I knew it had been a success. Though he answered my questions politely, I could tell he was anxious to take off. He was in a rush to join his new friends at the railing in front of the administrative building, the kids' favorite place to sit and talk. I was pleased he was fitting in easily and was obviously so excited to be around others who were blind like him.

The Michigan School for the Blind was founded in 1879, on a campus much like that of a small college. At its center stood the original, three-story building. When I'd been a pupil, administrative offices were housed on the first floor. Its upper floors served as the dormitory, with boys rooming on one side and girls living on the other. A house parent was assigned to each section and the school principal also lived there. The superintendent, Dr. Robert Thompson, his wife, Josephine, and their two children had a private, two-story home on campus.

Just a few years before I'd become a student, the school had been expanded substantially. The campus also included a library, a health center staffed twenty-four hours a day by an RN, plus a cafeteria building. There were separate buildings for the music department, arts, woodworking, and an auditorium.

Before taking Stevie to the school, I'd paid a visit to prepare for his arrival. Having been both a student and a student teacher there made my return comfortable, since I knew the campus and almost everyone on staff. It would have been difficult to go into an unfamiliar setting under such unusual circumstances and with a student I barely knew. If the faculty at the School for the Blind hadn't known me, I wouldn't have had their complete support and Stevie and I would have faced worrisome concerns.

What we were going to do for Stevie had never been done before at the School for the Blind. Instead of making one musically gifted student fit into the standard program, we were shaping Stevie's education around his talent and unusual career opportunity. To succeed, the faculty and I had to trust each other fully. They had to know that I was honest, capable, and that I wasn't a weirdo, pervert, alcoholic, racist or any other kind of crazy deviate. Returning to the School for the Blind as a tutor was like going home in some ways for me. It was a comfortable, trusting relationship and just one more thing that made my new job seem heaven-sent.

I explained to Stevie that we'd stay on campus as much as possible. As a residential facility, he'd live there and learn independent living skills along with his classroom lessons. Little did any of us know then that Stevie's blossoming financial security would allow him to have others take care of many chores and duties. Our concern was that, if his musical career didn't last, he'd develop the skills he'd need to competently and responsibly care for himself.

Stevie didn't ask many questions about the school, although I sensed he was nervous and somewhat scared. I remembered feeling the same way before my first day and tried to anticipate as many of his concerns as I could. But at thirteen, Stevie was still an exceptionally trusting, obedient boy who wanted to please. In many ways this wouldn't be much different than when his mother took him to elementary school for the first time. I stressed that I knew from my own experience how friendly the kids and teachers were. I assured him that if he had any problems at all, all he had to do was let me know, so Dr. Thompson and I could straighten them out.

By the time Motown employed me, the school year was already underway. On a cool, sunny September day barely a week after our trip to Chicago, Gene Shelby picked up Stevie, then came by my apartment. Two hours later we were in Lansing, and the School for the Blind had acquired the student who would become its most famous graduate.

First, we stopped by the office. Dr. Thompson, his secretary, the switchboard operator and others on the administrative staff were curious to meet this young musical genius they'd been hearing so much about. After quick introductions, we headed to the classroom where teacher Ginny Wiehn was expecting us.

Classes met in an old building with clean wooden floors whose shine had been long worn away ago by the feet of hundreds of blind children. It had the smell of an old school, too. Nearly a century of children's bodies, books and belongings gave the rooms a sense of comfort even the most pungent cleansers couldn't strip away.

The room was bright, airy and as attractive as in any public school. The biggest difference was the books—piles of braille books, stacks of braille books, and more and more braille books. Braille takes so much more space than print—one arithmetic book can fill eight or ten volumes in braille. There was a difference in sounds, too. In place of the scratching of pencils on paper, the clacking keys of braille writers or the soft punching of styluses against braille paper in slates broke the silence.

I went into the classroom with Stevie. Ginny introduced him to the other children, showed him to his seat, and went right back to the work they'd been doing when we arrived.

Stevie was treated as any new student would be, and no mention was made of Motown. Dr. Thompson had made it clear in an earlier staff meeting that Stevie's musical career was to be handled in a very low key manner. He was not to receive any special treatment. "We told teachers not to make Stevie special," he told me years later, "but we had to be smart enough to realize that he was special, and knew he was. So if we all accepted that, then maybe we could make things work."

I was supposed to participate in the class, helping out when needed. But I knew immediately that wasn't going to work. I just needed to drop Stevie off, get out of Ginny's hair and let her take care of things. There really was nothing for me to do in her classroom. And I knew it would be embarrassing for Stevie if I hovered over him all the time. None of the other kids had a specially assigned, personal teacher. Both of us would have felt self-conscious. I let Ginny know I'd be nearby and available if needed.

Later, I discovered another advantage to this arrangement. As I took on more and more road management responsibilities for Stevie, campus stays gave me much needed, uninterrupted time to handle those duties.

The first few days at the school passed quickly for both of us. Stevie was fascinated by his new surroundings and busy getting to know other kids and teachers who were blind. I had a plenty to do, too, preparing to take over Stevie's instruction when we left. I spent my time compiling lesson plans and collecting everything we'd need to handle schoolwork on the road.

Sighted students need little more than their books, paper and pencils to do homework. Tutoring Stevie off campus required an enormous amount of material and equipment. Dozens of the huge braille texts went with us. Talking books—recorded versions of books used in such classes as English literature, had to be played on a special machine. Stevie needed a typewriter, as typing is an important skill for blind people in communicating with the sighted. He also needed a Perkins Braille Writer, which looks something like a compacted typewriter and, after lugging its ten pound weight around, soon feels as heavy as concrete block. A lightweight slate and stylus allowed Stevie to take notes and write braille by hand on specially sized paper. For math, we carried along a cube board, which looks something like an oversized waffle. Plastic squares marked with braille numerals fit into its openings, making it possible to figure arithmetic as its done on paper.

While Stevie was in class, I also had time to roam the campus, reminiscing about my own days as a student. I knew his experiences would be vastly different from mine, but I was glad he'd have all the opportunities and camaraderie found at a residential school for the blind.

Pulling pranks on each other and trying to put things over our house parents were the most popular pastimes when I'd attended. Any time kids live in groups they find ways to entertain themselves—some more mischievous than others.

One year a bunch of us made homemade wine and rum in our dorm. One fellow made a concoction in gallon jugs by fermenting grapes in orange juice or lemonade. Those grapes turned green and swelled to the size of plums. It was the most god-awful tasting stuff, but we drank it and didn't care.

One day, word spread that the administration was on to us. In a panic, knowing we'd be raided any minute, one of the boys ran down the hall searching for a place to hide a gallon of freshly made wine. His brilliant solution was to pitch it down the dirty clothes chute. We could hear the explosion in the basement laundry from our dorm rooms three floors above. I'm still amazed we weren't all expelled. But none of us ever revealed the culprit, and soon we were back to making wine.

Another time, my roommate Dale Brockway and I noticed a trap door on the hallway ceiling, down past our house parent's desk. We took this as a challenge to sneak out at night. After waiting for our house parent to go to bed an hour after lights-out, we slipped down the hall. Dale climbed on my shoulders, pushed open the hatchway and pulled himself into the attic. He tied a rope around a roof truss and I used it to scamper up. We quietly replaced the trap door and tiptoed to another we'd found over the stairs in the center of the building. We had to be very careful, as our path was directly above the principal's room and we knew Mrs. DeBoer stayed up late. We made our way down to the basement, made sure the night watchman wasn't around, slipped out a window and high-tailed it across the shortest route off campus.

Dale and I never really had anything to do but wander around and smoke cigarettes on the many nights we escaped. The fun and excitement were in not getting caught.

There were other memories I recalled, too, some of which weren't quite so innocuous. Thinking back on those times, I was glad Motown and music gave Stevie's life plenty of excitement. He wouldn't need to get into trouble at school. Still, he did take part in shenanigans—such as when he and his buddies thought it extremely funny to slip pork onto a Jewish classmate's plate without his knowing, until he'd finished eating.

By the time Stevie became a student, the dormitory rooms had been replaced by cottages, each housing about twenty kids. Before sending the class off to lunch on Stevie's first day, his teacher asked another student to take him to Long House, where he'd live, to meet their house parents.

Like all the students, Stevie shared a bedroom, which opened onto a large recreation/living room. There, everyone gathered to watch and listen to television or play games. The two most popular were cards and checkers. Crazy 8's, Old Maid, gin rummy and even poker were played with cards that had both large print and braille. Specially designed checker boards had slots for shaped game pieces to fit into—squares were black and circles were red.

The only thing missing from the cottages was a kitchen. Lunch and dinner were served family-style in the main dining room. Learning to pass dishes and serve themselves were important parts of the students' daily living education and helped foster a close spirit on campus.

The dining room also gave the kids a way to gain some job experience. Allowed to work a few hours a week, students cleared tables, ran the dishwasher, and swept and mopped floors to earn extra money. As with teenagers everywhere, cash was king. It was spent on candy or snacks at the small school store or in the downtown Lansing shops a few blocks away, which always beckoned. Like his classmates, Stevie quickly discovered his weekly allowance had to be budgeted carefully. His Motown earnings still weren't much and, even after they were, I limited his pocket money. With all his needs taken care of, I felt it important he learn to discipline his spending just like any other teenager.

After lunch, everyone headed back to class. Even that walk was an experience in independence for Stevie. From the dining room, he traveled up four steps, turned right to follow the sidewalk past the administration building toward the physical education building. He then headed left past the health center, and turned once more, toward the classroom building. Although they received mobility training, Stevie and the other kids rarely bothered to use their white canes on campus. It seemed they always traveled in a herd, and someone in the group always knew where they were going and everyone else followed.

Several times during that first day, I went back to the classroom to peek in and make sure everything was all right. At the end of the day's classes, I waited outside to speak to both Stevie and his teacher. He fidgeted quietly while I chatted for a minute with Ginny Wiehn, who spoke well of her new student. Then I turned to him. "How did things go?"

"Fine. Can I go now?"

I had to laugh at his obvious desire to escape the grownups. "Okay, I'll see you both tomorrow."

Classes began promptly at eight-thirty in the morning. By eight-fifteen I was at the classroom door once more. I hadn't gone to bed until four o'clock that morning, but I wasn't going to sleep in just because others were responsible for Stevie. I wanted the faculty to see I was up, dressed and at work. Also, I wanted to make sure Stevie didn't try to slip back to the habits he'd developed at Fitzgerald Elementary, being tardy or missing classes.

I needn't have worried. The minute I could see the smile on his face, I knew Stevie felt right at home. But he'd barely had time to adjust to the school routine before Gene Shelby was back to drive us to Detroit.

Before the end of the week, Little Stevie Wonder would be performing at the Cow Palace in San Francisco and then at the Seattle World's Fair. But for the very first time, he could tour without causing guilty consciences at Motown. To do all the things that, until now, he'd had to sneak around to do.

Suddenly, the School for the Blind and I meant he could have an education and his career, too. New worlds opened. And he stepped into them very easily.

* * *

I don't know who was more fascinated by that first trip out West, Stevie or me. At thirteen, he was the headline star on a roster of national performers. Among the long list of acts were the Beach Boys, who'd had their first hit—*Surfin' Safari*—only a year earlier; Freddie "Boom Boom" Cannon, whose *Palisades Park* still invokes memories of summer for anyone who was young then; Ray Stevens, with the sly and inane comedy of *Ahab The Arab* and *Harry The Hairy Ape*; plus the brother/sister team of Nino Tempo and April Stevens, on the charts with their cover of the late-'30s hit *Deep Purple*.

The only other black performers on the bill were The Janettes. Their sole hit, *Sally Go 'Round The Roses*, is still one of the eeriest numbers to ever make the charts. One morning at breakfast, the four girls were at the table next to ours. They quizzed Stevie and me on what we thought the song was about. They giggled and teased us because neither of us had figured it out. Only later did I learn that was the song's intended allure. It was a mystery that never explained itself.

Here I was at twenty-five, glimpsing show business as few outsiders were privy to, and at a pivotal point in history. This was one of the few shows we'd do with both black and white performers. During that time in the 1960s, "white music" and "black music" were still distinctly separate. Elvis Presley had barely begun the crossover movement, creating quite an uproar by covering black rhythm and blues numbers.

But I credit Berry Gordy as the person who truly turned white America on to black talent. Motown's music also had a major impact, one often overlooked, on the civil rights movement of that period.

And there's no question Motown's stars delivered a message which eventually affected the international human rights movement. When Nelson Mandela was released after twenty-seven years as a political prisoner in South Africa—incarcerated the same year I became Stevie's teacher, he credited Motown for its influence on his thinking. And at an anti-apartheid rally in Detroit with Stevie, Mandela quoted a Marvin Gaye song when he reminded listeners that "too many of our brothers are dying."

Marvin Gaye, the Temptations, the Four Tops, Smokey Robinson, the Supremes, Martha and the Vandellas and others reached out and grabbed listeners of any color. Americans were ravenous for the exploding new sounds and sexuality of rock 'n' roll. Little Stevie Wonder exuded no sexuality at all that year—or for the next few. At that point, he was little more than a toy wonder to Motown and music.

56

During that first trip as Stevie's tutor, I quickly realized some things that set the course of my relationship with him. I could have approached my work strictly by the clock, with certain hours to be Stevie's teacher and the rest of my time as my own. Instead, curiosity pulled me backstage at the shows. I discovered that the singers and musicians were simply human, with the same qualities and foibles as the people filling the seats and cheering in front of the stage. I also watched Esther carefully. Her savvy and intelligence as she handled the day to day workings of a music tour taught me nuances of the business that I would soon put to good use.

I recognized that her care and concern for Stevie were sincere, but his career and well-being were only a small part of her Motown responsibilities. It was clear to me immediately that no one in particular was making sure Stevie got the rest he needed or that he ate regular and healthy meals. He'd been pulled away from his mother's watchful eye into a life surrounded by talented adults taking a shot at good times, fast money and fame. Esther alone wouldn't be able to shelter him from situations far beyond his age or maturity. And over the years there'd be plenty such opportunities to shield him from.

I think that's one of the things that go wrong for a lot of young stars. Two in particular stand out in my mind—one who became famous before Motown existed, the other made famous by Motown but who was taken from Berry's and Esther's attentive guidance.

Like Stevie, Frankie Lymon had been twelve years old when he started wowing Harlem crowds. And, like Stevie, "Little Frankie" was known as "the boy wonder." Fronting five singers called the Teenagers, Frankie's first big hit was *Why Do Fools Fall In Love*, a 1954 Top Ten hit that's still a golden oldie of early rock. At fifteen Frankie left the group, egotistically—and wrongly—believing himself too talented to need the others. At sixteen, backstage gossip claimed, his manager threw a big party to celebrate the fact that Frankie had contracted gonorrhea. At twenty-six, Frankie was dead of a drug overdose.

That kind of outcome might have been predicted for Stevie if he wasn't managed by people who really cared about him and his family. Sometimes, it was family who could contribute to problems. Michael

Jackson was the second boy wonder Gordy took to the top. Just as with Stevie, Motown protected the Jackson Five—Michael and his brothers—in many ways. But eventually, their father Joe broke with Motown and took over the group's management. What no one knew until many years later was how much Joe's drive for wealth harmed the entire family. Stevie had me as his watchful chaperone, while those directing the Jackson's held a vested interest in their income potential.

Maintaining integrity in the face of such temptations was difficult. Not long after becoming Stevie's teacher, I was offered a percentage of his earnings instead of a fixed salary. It could mean far more money than I was being paid as a teacher, but I knew it would only lead to trouble. It was imperative to me that Stevie, his mother, the Gordys and everyone at Motown knew my actions were based on what was best for him, not my own self-interest. And I was honest enough with myself to know the temptation might be too strong to resist. I wasn't earning a lot but, being young and single, I didn't need much either. Looking back from my financial position today, I sometimes wish I'd accepted the offer, although I've never regretted sticking to my principles and teaching Stevie to stick by his.

I'm sure one of the reasons Berry Gordy made such a success of Motown was because he could be incredibly tight with every dollar. That was part of the reason Stevie and I shared a room whenever we were on the road. The other reason was Stevie's age, compounded by his blindness. Sharing a room allowed me to teach him skills he'd need later, when he was old enough to spend nights alone. And the arrangement fostered my role as his guardian as well as his tutor.

Stevie's talent made him a challenge in many ways, but he was still a child and I quickly became protective of him. Dr. Thompson had cautioned me that Stevie could become "real heady" because of attention from fans and other performers. It was obviously true. Freddie Cannon treated Stevie like a kid brother, fussing over his bow tie before every performance. I knew his fans could be zealous in their attempts to track him down, and didn't want him exposed to possible harm before he knew how to take care of himself.

Right away I realized that I had to be concerned about protecting him physically. I was astounded, after the first show at the Cow Palace, by how wild the crowd was to get near Stevie, to touch him. It would have been an anxious situation even if Stevie could see, but I was even more fearful that he might be hurt because he couldn't react to visual information.

As I guided him out after that show, someone snatched him away from me, pushed him into a waiting car and slammed the door, nearly on his hand. All of a sudden, I understood that the crowds weren't the only thing I needed to protect him from. If Stevie was going to keep playing *Fingertips*, he certainly needed to keep his own, I figured.

So began my reputation as Stevie's mother hen. Off and on over the years I caught a lot of flack for it. On one trip to Washington, D.C., for a performance at Howard University when Stevie was seventeen, we did a fund-raiser at a public park where the crowd was particularly rowdy. We were forced to make a mad dash for the car and, as we sped away, I got into an argument with one of Berry's assistants.

"Oh, who cares about crowd control?" The guy only laughed at me. "We don't need it."

"Yeah?" I countered angrily. "And what happens if Stevie gets his hand caught in the car door because we don't have enough help?"

My concern proved valid. During the 1980s, Howard University planned to present Stevie with an honorary degree. But he canceled his appearance at the ceremony. Instead, he was at the hospital bedside of one of his guitar players—who'd lost his fingers in a car door.

Without A Song

"One day I was at the piano trying to teach him a tune and he was singing it, but he was playing another tune on the high end of the piano. I made him quit that. Then he started blowing another tune on the harmonica while he was playing a different one on the piano, and I took that away. Boy, he was mad. He was mad enough to cry."

— *Clarence Paul*

Stevie was polite and compliant as a student, but when it came to making music he didn't hesitate to let his personality come on strong.

Listening to the radio didn't require eyesight and like other kids his age, he loved rock 'n' roll. When he'd received a toy harmonica as a gift, Stevie quickly discovered that making music didn't require eyesight either. The more he played and sang around the neighborhood, the more he craved the attention and praise he attracted.

The fact that Stevie had natural talent is indisputable, but that didn't make him much different from thousands of other black kids in the ghettos of Detroit, New York, Boston, Philadelphia or any other city. During the early '60s, teenage guys with little else to do often hung out in groups on street corners to sing, putting their own spin on songs learned from the radio, and compete amongst themselves or others. For most of these *a cappella* doo-wop groups, it was a pleasant diversion from an otherwise bleak existence, a chance to gain neighborhood popularity ... and a great way to attract girls. Some lucky ones, like the Temptations, got their start toward stardom just this way.

In all likelihood, if he hadn't been blind, Stevie would never have amounted to much more than just another talented ghetto kid growing into an uncertain adulthood. But the blindness that cut him off from so much of the world opened another one to him. It gave him a reason to concentrate intensely on something he was good at. And music was the one way he could outshine his sighted friends. I firmly believe his blindness allowed Stevie to tap the genius which would otherwise have been lost in his struggle to survive.

Motown was less than a year old when the Miracles' Ronnie White and Pete "Pee Wee" Moore met Stevie. The Miracles were Motown's first big success group with *Got A Job*, a song Smokey Robinson co-wrote. The guys knew Gordy was always on the lookout for more talent that could attract national attention. Stevie's friend Gerald White kept hounding his cousin Ronnie to hear his buddy sing and play. Ronnie finally agreed and took Pee Wee along. Pee Wee never forgot how brash the kid was.

"He said 'I can sing badder than Smokey'," he told a writer years later, "which cracked us up. Until he actually started singing."

Stevie wowed the guys with his covers of some of their songs, such as *She's Not A Bad Girl*, and Marvin Gaye's *Mr. Sandman*. Ronnie passed their excitement about Stevie along to Motown talent scout Brian Holland, who invited the little kid to the studio. There, it was Stevie's harmonica which really impressed Berry. And the rest, as they say, is history.

Stevie started spending every extra minute hanging around the Hitsville studio, absorbing everything possible and trying to impress everyone he met. The men who made up Motown's studio group, loosely known as the Funk Brothers, were some of the greatest musicians to come out of the '40s and '50s—such as Thomas "Beans" Bowles, guitarists Joe Messina and Robert White, Earl Van Dyke on keyboard, pianist Joe Hunter, drummers Robert "Pistol" Allen and Benny Benjamin, and bass player Jamie Jamerson. To Stevie, these guys were a living hoard of fascinating knowledge and talent.

Benny Benjamin taught Stevie the drums. He'd sit Stevie on his lap and run the boy's hands around the drums so he'd know where each was. When Stevie mastered those, he insisted his drums always be set up exactly as Benny's were.

Gordy had tapped Beans for his experience in talent management as much as for his exceptional skill on saxophone and flute. Beans asked the other musicians to schedule an hour each week to work with Stevie, teaching him to play their various instruments.

"But after a while," Beans said, "we gave up on that because Stevie was always around anyway."

While flattered by the boy's attention and his real desire to learn, Stevie also made himself something of a nuisance.

"He'd bug the crap out of you," Beans said. "It was constantly 'Hey, man, how do you do this? Hey, what's that, man? How does that go, man?' When one of us got tired of him, we'd 'accidentally' run into one of the other guys and say 'Hey, Stevie wants to ask you something.' And while they were talking, you'd split."

There were several record producers at Motown, including Clarence, who worked with all the different artists. But only Clarence produced for Stevie, and I asked him why.

"Didn't nobody else want to be bothered," Clarence told me. "But I would listen to him. He'd start something on the piano and I'd show him something else to try. He started paying attention, because every time I'd tell him to do something, it sounded good. Then I started going in the studio, letting him do drums and organ and things like that."

Clarence also told me he was the one who came up with the name "Stevie Wonder" while Stevie was recording a tune called *Thank You, Mother*. Shortly after that, Clarence and Mickey Stevenson, who eventually ended up in charge of all recording at Motown, took Stevie along on a Sunday afternoon gig at a black resort called Shay Lake, near Saginaw. For the boy's first professional, but still unpaid, appearance, Mickey added the "Little" when he introduced Stevie on the "stage"— the bed of a pickup truck. I know Esther says her brother came up with the moniker, but even Berry admitted in his book, *To Be Loved*, that he doesn't really remember doing it.

One of the things Clarence found very exciting was how quickly Stevie caught on to both tunes and lyrics. Because Stevie read only some braille at that time and no one at Motown could write it, they had to find a way to work around his blindness in the studio. Clarence rigged a microphone to feed through a tape recorder into one of Stevie's earphones. Standing as far away from Stevie as possible in the tiny recording booth, Clarence whispered into his microphone, giving Stevie lyrics a line or two ahead. Through the other ear, he'd hear an already recorded music track to sing against.

It was a crude and imperfect method because the studio had to be totally free of any other sounds, and Clarence's whispering was often difficult for Stevie to understand. Shortly after I came on the scene, Motown's brilliant engineer Mike McLean devised a wiring system that allowed Clarence to stay in the control booth and still coach Stevie through his earphones. This significantly improved recording quality and speeded production.

"He could do it fast as I could read them to him," Clarence said. "And after he found out he could do that, he didn't try to learn lyrics. He just wanted to learn the melody."

Comparing Stevie's method to the other artists, Clarence claimed, "Most of the time, they wasn't half as good. Because they had to concentrate on reading. All he had to do was listen. He'd know the melody because I'd put the tune on tape."

It was one of Clarence's tunes that first took Stevie to the top of the charts. He and Hank Cosby had written *Fingertips* as a jazz instrumental. They asked Beans Bowles to add a flute line to the melody. With Stevie on bongos for its first recording, it turned into a great ensemble number. At a show at Chicago's Regal Theater, Beans let Stevie and his bongos join the other musicians. Stevie soon was messing with the number on piano and organ, so it seemed a good idea to include it on his album *The Twelve-Year-Old Genius*.

At a later engagement at the Regal, which Motown was recording live, Stevie bugged Clarence through two shows to let him do a harmonica solo on *Fingertips*.

Winehead Willie, Motown's popular emcee, finally told Clarence in exasperation, "Man, you better might as well let him play. He can't do nothin'. What's he gonna do?"

Clarence gave in and soon found out just what Stevie was going to do. Backing the band on bongos, Stevie got the crowd to clapping. As usual. Then he switched to harmonica for the solo. As planned. The band finished the song and left the stage. But not Stevie. He kept right on playing. Next thing Clarence knew, Stevie was yelling to the crowd, "Everybody say 'Yeah!' " And the crowd roared back.

"Man, I'd never heard noise so loud," Clarence said. "It scared me. I picked him up and took him off the stage. But them kids were hollering and he wanted back on stage. He jumped right back out there."

Mary Wells' band was on stage by then, getting ready for her appearance. Stevie kept yelling, "Everybody say 'Yeah!' ", the audience kept screaming back, and he kept wailing on the harmonica. Figuring there wasn't much they could do to stop him, the band decided to join in.

Caught on the live tape of the show was bass player Joe Swift yelling over the crowd, "What key? What key?" Trumpet player Herbie Williams hollered back, "What do you care? You play everything in the same key anyway!"

Fingertips Part 2 had just been created. And Stevie clearly had made his point to Clarence about wanting more creative input.

But at just thirteen, Stevie didn't have much more to offer than a bit of a lyric here or a strand of melody there on the tunes Clarence and a few others were writing for him. Whenever we traveled, Clarence and Stevie constantly played with song ideas.

From the start, I couldn't resist tossing in my opinions. Clarence knew about the contract my friend Tony Juliano and I had with the Nashville music publisher. While in college, Tony and I and another friend, Bill Palmer, got a bar band to help us tape a song I'd written— *Purple Raindrops*. When Clarence asked to see something I had done, that's what I handed him. So the "creative team" of Paul and Wonder expanded to Paul, Wonder and Hull.

Nearly three years would pass after *Fingertips* before Stevie had another chart topper. His talent never failed to pull the crowds, but no one at Motown seemed as concerned as Clarence and I about finding Stevie another hit. He felt Gordy and Motown were more interested in the Supremes, the Temptations, Marvin Gaye, Smokey Robinson and the Miracles than in him. Stevie seemed relegated to doing "nice" music, such as the album of standards cut with the Chicago Symphony,

Clarence's *La La La La La* or *Castles In The Sand*, one of the syrupy numbers he'd had to perform in *Muscle Beach Party*. Some of his songs were better and the records did fairly well—*Workout, Stevie, Workout*; *Hey Harmonica Man* and *High Heel Sneakers*. The flip side of *High Heel Sneakers* was especially important to me—*Music Talk* was the first tune I shared song writing credit on.

Stevie increasingly resented Motown's nonchalant attitude toward his career and, frankly, he had every right to feel that way. Motown hadn't capitalized on his unprecedented achievement of having a single and an album simultaneously at No. 1 on the charts. After that, it seemed no one could—or would—come up with another major hit for him. During the next three years with no big hits, I realized some of Stevie's cynicism typical of adolescence, but I really was concerned about the bitterness Motown's lack of attention fueled in him. By then, Clarence was no longer Stevie's music director, which put an end to their creative relationship. Nobody else was interested in giving Stevie the concentrated attention Clarence had. Every chance I got I pushed the writers to work on tunes for Stevie, but still nothing happened.

Eventually, Gordy realized he couldn't let Stevie's career languish any longer. Hank Cosby and Sylvia Moy, a former school teacher who'd joined Motown's stable of writers, not-so-enthusiastically agreed to take on the duty. Off and on over the years, they'd written a few tunes for him , fitting the work in between writing smash hits for other Motown stars. But finally, finally, something clicked. With Stevie's contribution, Sylvia and Hank wrote *Uptight (Everything's Alright)*. Stevie recorded my song *Purple Raindrops* as the flip side of that single, which would become his second No. 1 hit.

Stevie also found those years difficult because he wanted so badly to become a superstar like others he saw around him in Motown. He wanted quick fortune and more of the fame he'd tasted with *Fingertips*. Without Motown's active interest and support, he didn't get what he wanted. But as the Rolling Stones later sang, "You may not always get what you want, but you always get what you need." What Stevie needed was time to mature, and to learn from the rich musical history and talent surrounding him.

Clarence was one of the few adults in Motown willing to listen to the youngster's creative suggestions, especially in the very early days. Clarence's musical tutoring did much to give Stevie the solid footing he needed to develop his personal style in both music and lyrics. Even as a very young teen, he had a unique style others couldn't imitate. He wanted more artistic freedom but still needed the grounding and training that Clarence put him through. He needed someone like Clarence to say, "No, man, you gotta sing the melody. You're not singing the melody, you're singing all around it. You think it's cute but that's not the way the audience is gonna want to hear it. I know. I've been out there for twenty years. Listen to me."

So Stevie listened, soaking up as much as possible. Hanging around the studio, it was Clarence who'd let him mess around on various instruments. He played, or tried to play, anything he got his hands on. He'd feel around the room until he'd come across an instrument he couldn't recognize. "'What's this?'" Clarence said Stevie would ask. "Then he'd slay that."

Even though Stevie wasn't getting exactly what he wanted from Motown, he usually remained cooperative with the musical direction he was given. Once in a while, though, he'd get surly and argue points. Times like that, I turned into more of a Dutch uncle than teacher, letting him know I thought he was out of line. I'd remind him to just be cool and try what was being suggested, because the people he was working with really did know more than he.

"He'd get ticked off," Clarence said, "but he'd end up doing it because that was the only way. Everybody else there did, and they were getting their records out by doing what people said to do."

What I found really interesting, though, was that Stevie's drive for recognition virtually disappeared at the School for the Blind. There, he was in choir and orchestra and studied music theory. Anything but shy in the Motown studios, at school he was almost the opposite. He enjoyed having his classmates know who he was but never used his fame to manipulate them. Instead of pushing his creativity on those around him, he was simply another student doing as he was told by the choir director or orchestra leader.

Stevie took part in musical programs whenever it was possible for us to arrange his schedule to coincide with the school shows. Only once, during the Christmas program in 1964, did he solo. The feeling he invoked singing *Ave Maria* created a spiritual hush in the audience that's still talked about today by those who heard him. His voice literally raised the goosebumps on everyone.

Classes at the school exposed Stevie to a much wider range of material, particularly classical, than most of the others at Motown were trained in. I think this base of knowledge allowed him to develop his staying power as a creative talent. Leaving Detroit and the road for the School for the Blind also gave Stevie much-needed physical, emotional and mental breaks from the rigorous schedule required by his career and Motown. On campus, Stevie could let his mind synthesize what he was learning as both a professional and as a student.

While Dr. Thompson, the other teachers and I did everything we could to keep Stevie's time at school separate from his career, I did capitalize on his fame in one way to benefit his schoolmates. I set up occasional music clinics where Stevie jammed with other musicians. I'd gotten the idea from week-long music clinics hosted by band leader Stan Kenton at Michigan State University. He'd bring his band in to conduct student workshops and do campus concerts. For years, it was an event everyone in Lansing looked forward to.

When I could, I'd get some of the Motown studio musicians, like Earl Van Dyke, Pistol Allen, Joe White and Jamie Jamerson to come up to the school for clinics. Their own schedules made it hard to arrange, so I started scouting local bands. All I had to do was ask, "How'd you like to spend a few hours working with Stevie Wonder?" Never failed.

But the most important reason for the clinics was to give the school's music students and choir members hands-on experience working with Stevie and other professional or accomplished musicians. The local band members loved it and so did the other kids, who got their own personal and private Stevie Wonder concerts.

Uptight

*"Stevie talks with excitement of the great places he has
'seen' throughout his travels ... the teenager does 'see'
a great deal—through his other senses."*
— *The Grand Rapids Press*

As Stevie's ease on stage grew, so did rumors among his fans that he
wasn't really blind. A different rumor circulated through Motown—
that surgery could give Stevie the eyesight that he'd never had. Even
Clarence Paul asked me if it was true.

Stevie and I had discussed the fact that nothing could be done about
his blindness, and I thought such notions had been dispelled. In Paris, I
discovered Stevie still didn't, or didn't want to, believe me.

Rock 'n' roll, which had captured the ears and hearts of American
and British teenagers, was beginning to explode in popularity throughout
Europe. Motown, ever poised to reach out to new fans, found in Stevie it
had just what the French youth wanted.

"Little Stevie Wonder" was Motown's first emissary to Paris as the
headline star of a December 1963 show at the Olympia Theater. The only
other American on the bill was Dionne Warwick, also just beginning her
singing career. Marcel Marceau performed, as did six or eight other
outstanding acts gathered from around Europe. Out of all of our travels,
that's the trip that stands out in my mind.

With Ardena Johnston's help, Lula filed the paperwork to get
passports for Stevie and herself. My well-stamped passport was ready to
go, and I looked forward to the interesting educational opportunities
travel would offer Stevie. But on the day we picked up the passports, I
was the one who got the first lesson.

By then, I'd been with Stevie a few months. I knew what his name was—and how to spell it correctly. I'd learned that his legal name was Stephen Judkins. It was the name I'd registered him under at the School for the Blind. It was the name he put on all his school papers. That's how he was introduced, and that was the name he answered to.

"What's the name?" asked the lady at the government office when we picked up the passports. My wandering thoughts focused abruptly as Lula answered, "Steveland Morris."

It was a name I'd never heard before. I did my best to cover my surprise and was glad Stevie couldn't see my reaction. His face was an almost unreadable mask, but a glimmer of emotion told me that he must have just recently learned this new name and was still adjusting to the knowledge. It was one more indication his life was taking him in directions he'd never anticipated.

Dealing with the changes wrought by his developing career only compounded the typical growing pains of adolescence. Stevie wasn't completely used to Motown's demands and expectation, or my being his constant companion. All in all, Stevie's life was in a constant state of flux.

That created a lot of anxiety for him, and Stevie's tension kept me tense, too. The fact that Lula would be with us on the Paris trip only increased the pressure I felt. Whenever Lula traveled with us, everyone was apprehensive. The day I learned she'd be along, I jokingly told Esther, "Gee, I don't think I'm going to be able to make this trip."

She looked at me, dead serious, and growled, "Oh, yes, you are."

We all dreaded dealing with Lula, because Lula could be explosive. Intimidated by the money and power Motown represented, she was extremely sensitive and quick to become defensive. And when Lula blew up, it didn't matter where she was and or who was around. It would have been easier to deal with her if I'd been able to predict when she was likely to lose her temper. But no one ever knew what might set her off.

The first time I saw Lula in high action was one day when Stevie and I were doing school work at his house. We were in the sun room, with a bay window overlooking the front walk. A man came up the steps and knocked. Since Lula was busy elsewhere, I answered the door and asked the gentleman to wait. I told Lula that someone from a furniture store wanted to see her about a bill, then returned to Stevie's lesson.

Next thing I knew, Lula was loudly, angrily and quite explicitly telling the man exactly where he could go, how he could get there and what he could do with himself once he arrived. Stevie and I listened to the commotion in surprised silence. Peering out the window, I watched her try to bodily throw the guy off the stoop. He stumbled down the steps and high-tailed it out of the neighborhood without so much as a parting word.

Looking back at Stevie, I noticed him wrenching at a clump of his hair. It was a nervous compulsion I'd been noticing more often. He'd managed to pluck bald a spot the size of a dime, and it pained me to realize how greatly Lula's volatility impacted him.

"You know," I said lightly as I opened my teaching manual again, "I don't think your mother likes that man very much."

Stevie's nervous hair twisting gave way to a conspiratorial giggle as we went back to work.

(Years later, Stevie was performing at the Uptown Theater in Philadelphia. My wedding was coming up and I had to return to Detroit, so Lula came out to be with her seventeen year old son. After I returned from my honeymoon, one of the crew told me she'd gotten angry at someone and hauled a pistol out of her purse. All I could think was, "Great! My kid's in the room and his mom's waving a gun around!" I had no way of knowing whether it was true, and wouldn't have put it past someone to make up such a story. But I had to give the story credence because I knew Lula was not a woman to be messed with.)

When it was time to leave for the Paris trip, Stevie and I were in California doing promotional appearances, working on his new album *Castles In The Sand*, and talking with American International Productions about his first movie appearance. From there, we flew to New York where we met Esther, Lula and Wade Marcus, who'd be Stevie's musical director for the show.

Stevie and I had been away from home for nearly two weeks by then and would be in Paris another two. Having learned to travel as light as possible, we each had one large suitcase, plus a trunk for Stevie's school materials and stage costumes. Wade, also a seasoned traveler, carried a single suitcase and his trombone. When we all gathered at the airport, I took one look at the mountainous pile of luggage and trunks and bags and suitcases surrounding Lula and Esther and wondered if they'd left *anything* home.

As exciting as it was for Stevie to make his first journey to Europe as the top billed star on an international roster, he struggled with so much frustration on that trip. Lula was still very distrustful of Motown. More and more, so was Stevie, who was beginning to feel ignored in favor of other Motown acts. He hadn't had a decent hit since *Fingertips*. All these things fueled the cynicism and moodiness that was just a part of being a teenager.

And he really was tired of being treated like a kid and being pitied for his blindness. The first news article in a Paris paper only added to his vexation. We'd been pleased to be greeted at Orly Airport by the show's promoter, a number of fans, and several members of the press. As usual, I helped guide Stevie's hand as he signed autographs. But our pleasure over the turnout turned to disgust the next day. A reporter for the major newspaper reported that "Little Stevie Wonder was so nervous upon his arrival that his manager had to steady his hand while he signed autographs."

Stevie's voice still hadn't found its true register, which was also frustrating. On top of that, he was experiencing physical discomfort whenever he spoke or sang, and we were all worried about his health. (After we returned home, doctors discovered two nodules on his vocal chords and underwent surgery; for two weeks he was forced to remain totally silent. Even then, the doctors couldn't say how the surgery might effect his voice. It was a time of almost more emotional strain than Stevie could handle.)

Fortunately, some of his numbers in Paris were instrumentals. Also, Wade was an excellent arranger who tried to keep the music rewritten to fit Stevie's changing vocal range. Still, the thirteen-year-old was struggling and it was obvious in his act. He just wasn't having the impact and the audience didn't respond the way we were accustomed. We'd all talked about it during the first few shows, but hadn't reached a conclusion about what to do.

On the third day, Christmas Eve, the show's promoter dropped in. Out of the clear blue, Wade announced, "Stevie's having trouble hitting the high notes. We don't want to him to close the show anymore. I'd like you to move him to an earlier spot."

This was news to me. But I figured Wade and Esther had decided this was best. That evening, Esther admitted Wade's decision surprised her, too. She told me she didn't agree, because Berry insisted that the headliner, the star of the show, was always the closing act. She wasn't sure Wade had done the right thing, but she also wasn't about to embarrass him in front of the promoter.

Stevie was particularly upset by Wade's decision. He took it as confirmation that "everyone" at Motown was against him. And since Lula and I were the ones he spent most of his time with, we received the brunt of his frustration.

Christmas day came and, as always, there was a show to do. When it was time to meet Stevie in the room he and his mom shared, I carried along the gift I'd bought Lula. I knew she was still trying to determine whether she could trust me. When I presented her with the magnum of sparkling burgundy wine, I knew she was genuinely pleased by the way she ooh-ed and aah-ed.

"Let me see it," Stevie said.

I carried it over to where he stood near the end of the bed and handed it to him. As he reached for the heavy bottle, it slipped from his fingers and crashed onto my foot.

"I saw that!" Lula snapped, and unleashed a thorough tongue-lashing on her son's ears.

Through the excruciating, throbbing pain I kept repeating, "Lula, it was an accident."

"No!" Lula turned her blazing eyes on me. "He did that on purpose."

From the look on Stevie's face and his stance, I realized she was absolutely right. He really had dropped the bottle intentionally, though I don't think he expected it would break my toe. He was making it clear to me that he wasn't impressed with my gift to his mother, nor her pleasure at receiving it. Even though the bottle hadn't broken, as he'd probably hoped, his attitude also made it clear that he wasn't too thrilled with Lula then, either.

Stevie and I were both silent as we rode the elevator down to the lobby to wait for our ride to the theater. Trying my best to ignore the incredible pain, I wondered if I was ever going to get control of the downward spiral surrounding me. There was so much paranoia and distrust being shown by both Stevie and Lula that I questioned whether I could continue as his teacher.

"Stevie," I finally said, "we've got to work this out. I'm your teacher and I'm supposed to be in charge. I'm tired of your arrogance and making everything a struggle. It's your choice. You can change your attitude or I'm just going to say to heck with it. I'm not going to invest my life in a situation that's not going to work."

Stevie said absolutely nothing. But I wasn't about to let the subject drop.

"If you're not interested in my helping you get through school, I've got my own life to live. My folks raised me to believe that I can be anything I want to be. Even president of the United States. I'm young enough to go after any career I want. What I don't want is to waste my time with you."

"You? President of the United States?" His smirk and the snide tone of voice made it clear his comment was meant to be rude.

For the first time, I became truly angry with Stevie. If he'd been my child, I thought, I'd have turned him over my knee. I barely spoke to him for the rest of that night.

But I did talk to Esther. I made it clear I was fed up. Either he shaped up or I was out as soon as this trip was over. My time and energy were being wasted, and putting up with the situation wouldn't do him or me one bit of good.

Esther understood the implications very clearly. It hadn't been easy to find a suitable tutor to begin with. Without a tutor, Stevie couldn't travel, which would affect his career. The Gordy's were well aware of Stevie's potential and the impact his stardom meant for Motown. If they were forced to release Stevie for the sake of his education, all the plans and dreams for Stevie's future would be cut short. And Stevie's and Lula's hopes of ever leaving the ghetto would be dashed.

I don't know what took place after I made it clear that either I was in control or I was gone. I can only assume Esther had a very serious talk with Lula and probably with Stevie, because the situation improved immediately and dramatically. Before, Lula only went through the motions of supporting me as his teacher. Now, she seemed to fully understand the opportunities I was able to offer Stevie and her support became genuine. She began trusting me to do what was best for her son, and relying on me when he or one of her other children had a problem.

Paris did nothing to subdue Lula's forceful personality toward others, though. One day Stevie, Esther, Lula and I were outside our hotel trying to flag down a taxi. So were several other people. A cab pulled up, but before we could reach it, it was taken.

We flagged a second cab, only to have others rush past us to get it.

The third time that happened, we did some muttering about how the Parisians could teach pushy New Yorkers a thing or two.

A fourth cab pulled up. A well dressed French woman leaped in. By then, Lula had had enough. She grabbed the door, swung it open and reached inside. Dragging the stunned woman out by the shoulder, Lula growled, "Honey, this is *my* cab!" We got in and rode off, leaving the poor lady standing open-mouthed at the curb.

Feeling responsible for Lula as well as Stevie during long hours backstage only increased the pressures I felt on that trip. When Lula was with us, I always felt I had to entertain her and keep a conversation going. But because she and Stevie shared a hotel room, it meant I could have an occasional break to enjoy some of the local night life.

An American group called The Rockin' Robins was popular in Paris at that time. Their manager came to see Stevie's show and invited us to see their act the next night. At thirteen, Stevie was too young to attend, so he and Lula stayed behind while Wade, Esther and I headed out for a much anticipated good time.

In show business, managers who are personally invited to a show are usually treated as guests of the house. When we arrived at the club, we learned that the fellow who'd invited us wasn't there. But the Rockin' Robins were playing, so we went on in. Next, we discovered that we'd have to pay for our cover charges and drinks, neither of which we had expected.

None of us was carrying much money but, still, this was okay. While we watched the show, we each drank two beers, figuring we could easily afford that. After all, a beer back in the States cost, at most, fifty cents. When the waitress brought our tab, we discovered we'd been charged nearly sixty dollars for six beers!

We'd had to deal with some minor aggravations before where the French tried to take advantage of us as Americans, but this was outrageous. After a whispered conversation, we decided to leave what we thought the drinks were worth and try to get out without making a scene.

There was a slight problem, though. We'd come straight from the theater. Wade, who was part of Stevie's band, had brought his trombone and checked it in the coatroom. We knew as soon as he claimed his horn, someone would be at our table to collect our tab.

Wade meandered toward the coatroom. A minute later, Esther and I hurried toward the door to meet him. The maitre d' quickly figured what was up. Glowering, he jumped in front of us.

"You did not pay your bill," he said menacingly.

"Yes, we did," I said, my voice as belligerent as his. "We paid what the drinks were worth."

"Either you pay the rest of the bill," he threatened, "or I will call the police."

"*You* call the police?" Now, my voice was loud enough to be heard throughout the entire club. "Where's the phone? *I'll* call the police!"

I don't know why I decided to be our spokesman, and I don't know what I would have done if he had handed me a phone. I was just trying to embarrass him. It worked. He let us go.

* * *

That entire trip was fraught with problems. But the troubles with Stevie's voice, Lula's unpredictable nature, and the nightclub incident were completely eclipsed by something far worse.

A London newspaper sent a reporter to spend a few days with us. A gorgeous, sexy young black woman, she thoroughly charmed us all. As it turned out, she was about as charming as a black widow spider. While she was flirting with Wade and me and buttering up Esther, she was ensnaring Stevie in a web of rumors that fed his distrust of Motown. I began to suspect her motives when Stevie asked me one day why he couldn't have the operation to get his sight back.

"What operation? What are your talking about?" I'd heard that kind of rumor back in Detroit from Clarence, and had set him straight.

The reporter, Stevie explained, told him there was an operation to restore his eyesight. "But Esther won't allow it," he said, "because if I could see, then I wouldn't be a star for Motown. And they won't make money off me."

I was outraged that the woman could be so cruel as to lie like that. My heart went out to Stevie as I gently explained what he already really knew—there simply was no medical procedure to restore his sight.

Not much later, all of us were in a meeting with the reporter. Esther excused herself for a moment. As soon as the door closed behind her, the reporter turned to Stevie.

"I don't like her," she said. "Why do you let her tell you what to do? She's not your mother. Why should you trust her? She really doesn't care about you. She just wants Motown to make money off you."

I was stunned and said absolutely nothing. Neither did Wade nor Lula, and Stevie never directly answered the challenge. Esther returned and the reporter easily slipped back to an earlier conversation. But my discomfort continued to increase as I sensed a change in Esther, who now seemed encased in ice.

That night, all of us met for dinner. Again, the air was tense. Stevie was surly. Lula was cross with Esther. Esther, normally warm and outgoing, was more curt than I'd ever seen her. It was hard to have any appetite in that kind of atmosphere.

The next day, the reporter returned to London and I discovered the reason for Esther's barely submerged rage. After she'd left the room the previous day, she realized she'd forgotten something. As she'd reached for the door, she overheard a comment that caused her to stop and listen. She'd listened to every disparaging remark the young woman had made.

"Ted," she said, "you and Wade let that woman walk all over you just because she was sexy."

I knew she was right. And although Esther never said so, I knew I should have acted quickly to put an end to the woman's manipulations.

* * *

But on top of all the troubles, Stevie's education remained my primary concern. And for both of us, the field trips we took in Paris provided our best memories.

Like most kids his age, social studies and history were difficult book subjects for Stevie to grasp or really care about. But traveling around the world brought books and history to life for Stevie.

In every foreign country we visited over the years, I'd take Stevie to a school for the blind to meet other students and learn about their educational and cultural experiences. The very first one we visited was *Le Institut National Pour L'Aveugle*—the National Institute for the Blind in Paris. There, Stevie sat at the table where Louis Braille had studied more than a hundred years before. Louis Braille was fifteen, barely two years older than Stevie then, when he began devising the complicated system of raised dots that made reading possible for Stevie and millions of other blind people. Though we spent little more than an hour at the school on a dreary, lonely day during the Christmas holiday break, it created a link that bonded Stevie with both the past and the future.

Although Louis Braille revolutionized education for the blind, their career opportunities remained as limited as ever. When I was a child, most blind people in the United States were expected to cane chairs, make brooms or tune pianos. In France, we discovered it wasn't much different. At the dark and depressing school for the blind, it seemed every blind person was expected to become a church organist or, just like at home, a piano tuner.

Visits to other schools made Stevie aware that Motown's support of his talent meant his future could far exceed what an "ordinary" blind person might look forward to. As someone with a severe visual impairment, I knew there was much more to life than what was offered most blind people. And visits such as these allowed me to relate my own experiences, concerns and hopes to Stevie. Through everything we did, I tried to pass along the confidence and optimism that I had for both our futures.

It simply never crossed my mind that I shouldn't expose Stevie to every experience possible. After all, eyesight is only one way to experience thought-provoking wonders. At the Louvre, even though he couldn't see the pictures, I wanted him to know about the art and the artists, to know what it was like to be in the world's most famous gallery. We absorbed the majestic, spiritual aura permeating the ancient cathedral of Notre Dame.

Later, when we traveled to the Netherlands, just because he couldn't see the ships was no reason to miss touring Rotterdam harbor. Stevie certainly understood descriptions of the fantastically large ships gathered there from all over the world. He absorbed the sounds and the smells as cargo was unloaded and loaded and the ships were piloted back to sea. Before we visited Amsterdam, Stevie read *The Diary of Anne Frank*. But it was grasping the doorknobs that her hands had turned, brushing his fingers over the walls she and her family hid behind during World War II that made her life, like Louis Braille's, alive for him.

It was the same everywhere our years of travel took us. In Mexico, surrounded by lush mountain jungle smells and sounds, Aztec ruins made real a civilization that had disappeared four hundred years earlier. Echoes expressed the immensity of St. Peter's Basilica in Rome. He felt the columns and doors and grasped their textural structure and size, and told me he pictured everything except the color of the interior. The experience fed Stevie's awareness of the revered ground we stood on.

Sighted people often thought it so odd that I'd take my blind student on excursions. But I knew the importance of all the information Stevie could absorb through all his senses—there is so much more to experience in life than just the visual. And even as a teen, he had a sensitivity and empathy unusual for a person of any age. Each of these field trips made a lasting, emotional impact on him.

We tried to share those experiences with his classmates at the Michigan School for the Blind. When he had given them a report on our Delaware River canoe trip, I realized none of the students knew what a canoe was. I found a toy canoe for them to touch, and was delighted to see the flash of understanding as they grasped what Stevie talked about. I taught him that way often, too. Before visiting the Eiffel Tower, Stevie learned about the structure through a souvenir model. And our tape recorder was a great way to capture the sounds of different places, from anyplace we could record them, for his classmates back home. The next year, in Liverpool, Stevie and I leaned way out our open hotel window to record the sounds of the traffic passing ten floors below.

But our field trips could create dilemmas that we later recalled with humor. Our visit to the gardens at Versailles is indelibly imprinted in my memory as one such occasion. Halfway through the guided tour, Stevie had to go to the bathroom so bad he couldn't stand it. I didn't know what to do, so we just broke away from the group and headed down the street to find any place with a bathroom.

After blocks and blocks of running, with Stevie becoming more and more uncomfortable, we finally came to a restaurant. But the waiter didn't speak English and we didn't speak French, so it took forever to communicate the now-desperate need. We should have taken some lessons from Marcel Marceau, the famous mime who was on the theater program with us during that trip. If he'd seen us trying to show the waiter what we needed, Marcel could have added a hilarious new segment to his act.

So no matter where his career took us, Stevie and I always "blindly" and blithely enjoyed being the tourists we were. As are most major European cities, Paris is a great place for people who don't drive. Over our ten day visit for that Olympia Theater show, we went everywhere—by subway, bus, cab or on foot.

We strolled around the city filling our senses with its sounds and scents. We dined at fine restaurants and local cafes, sampling new foods. Stevie was particularly intrigued by the unheated bistros and cafés—he thought it so odd that diners sat outside in their winter coats while they ate.

Everywhere we went, we talked about the French culture, what was going on in Vietnam and how the French had fought there long before our own country became embroiled in that war. We talked about the racial problems at home and how they didn't seem to exist in Paris. We tried hard to understand why it was so different in America.

And we glimpsed the troubled future terrorism would bring to the world. As was happening in the States, French college students were beginning to demonstrate against their government; just days after we shopped at a fine department store, it was damaged in one of the city's first bombings.

Wherever we traveled, everything we did was always a combination of learning and fun, mostly because both of us were curious about other people. By letting him see how others around the world lived, it helped me teach him that, despite the problems in the United States, we had a lot to be grateful for.

Stevie was always fascinated by people from other countries. And it was on this trip that I discovered his talent for foreign languages. I was surprised how quickly he picked up phrases, and how he'd use them as often as he could. (When Stevie was seventeen, he was chatting with Bill Cosby a few weeks before the Motown Revue left for Japan. Bill was always interested in Stevie's education and urging him to strive. "The Japanese will really be impressed if you can talk to them," Bill told him. "Tell Ted to teach you to speak Japanese before you go." I never knew if Bill was joking or if he thought I could learn it that fast, too!)

Even meeting people backstage fed his education. No matter who they were or what they did, Stevie's natural curiosity drew out whatever he could learn from them. Working around foreign musicians, such as the fantastic house band at the Olympia, and the Afghan group that shared the bill, exposed him to new creative ideas and different philosophies.

Unless we were with the Revue's huge entourage, we hired our own bands for Stevie's performances on the road. Musicians in England, France, Italy or Japan taught Stevie as much about people as they did about music. Today, I know his originality in musical expression and his sincere human concern express the cultural depth he gained from that exposure.

Lighting The Fire

*"In the early years, Stevie kept that stage too hot. Mary
Wells didn't want to go on behind him and Marvin Gaye
didn't want to go on behind him. The Supremes didn't want
to go behind him. Not even when they were No. 1."*
—Gene Shelby

Stevie's classmates at the School for the Blind were the only ones able
to enjoy his talent for free. Berry Gordy, who'd started out on a shoe
string (and a thin shoe string, at that), knew the best way to build
Motown was to keep its performers in front of paying fans. That meant
hitting the road, taking sizzling glamour and hot tunes wherever a
promoter wanted.

People seem to think that talent grew on trees in Detroit in the '60s
because Motown had so many homegrown stars. Maybe there was some
harmonic convergence that delivered so much truly outstanding talent
into a single generation there. More likely, I think the talent exists
everywhere. The difference was Berry and Motown, giving those kids
the chance to do something with their gifts.

Gordy had the entrepreneurial streak, strong desire and street smarts
needed to create a musical dynasty. If he'd started Motown after
establishing a career in the music industry, things would have turned out
much differently. The old house on West Grand Boulevard, which he
made into the Hitsville studio, was a place where these kids could hang
around and play at their music. With Motown's nurturing, a lot of their
talent flourished.

Most of the Gordy family was involved in Motown then and all
provided strong guidance. Especially Pop Gordy, who's No. 1 rule was

that family took care of each other. For many of the young people who found their way to Hitsville, the Gordys became the family they hadn't had at home.

There was fun and excitement at Motown. I'd often find Stevie on the front porch or out on the lawn wrestling around with one of the Temptations or the Contours, Clarence Paul or whoever else had time to play. It wasn't the sort of atmosphere that would have been accepted in well established, structured companies such as Atlantic records or RCA.

"If Stevie Wonder had wandered into Capitol records in California," Esther told me once, "they'd probably have thrown the kid out."

I'm sure she was right.

Every cent Motown generated in those early years went right back into the business. New tunes and fabulous stage costumes were investments. Luxury travel was a frivolous expense. Looking like we all lived the high life was an image presented to the fans. Off stage, on the road, life was anything but.

When I hear Smokey Robinson's smooth voice on the radio or see gorgeous Diana Ross or Stevie on TV, I often think of them at the back of a bus. Not inside—outside. That's still a vivid picture in my mind—all of us out there pushing a stalled bus to get it going again. On every single trip it seemed the vehicle would break down eventually or not start. So many times we'd often come out of a show and have to ask, "Where's the bus?" "It's two blocks away," would come the answer. "We had to park on a hill so we can roll down to get it started."

We spent a lot of time waiting along side of the road for our rides to be fixed. It wasn't particularly humorous back then. We were tired, hot, sweaty and hungry and usually had hundreds of miles left to go. But getting to the next gig was part of our job, no matter what it took.

Stevie and I weren't part of the first long Motown Revue in 1962, but we were on every one after that. They usually lasted for weeks—up to thirty cities in thirty nights, with as many as four shows a day on Saturdays and Sundays.

At the start of each Motown Revue, all of us buzzed on sheer excitement. The bus would be scheduled to leave Detroit in the morning around nine-thirty. By nine-twenty, I made sure Stevie and I were seated and settled. Nine-thirty would come and go. The bus driver would begin checking his watch.

Eventually, a few others straggled on board. Martha Reeves and the Vandellas. The Supremes with Diana Ross, Mary Wilson and Flo Ballard. The Temptations. The Four Tops. The Contours. Smokey Robinson and The Miracles. Mary Wells. Then Choker Campbell and his band. Comic ventriloquist Willy Tyler brought his dummy. Comedian Bill Murray, our emcee, arrived. Beans Bowles, too, who was in charge of road management. Stevie's musical director, Clarence Paul, finally showed up. Sometimes Esther or Berry came along. And then, just about when everyone had given up hope of his showing, Marvin Gaye would join us. (Once, he didn't. A white-knuckle flyer, he simply refused to board the plane, and no one could talk him into it.)

Fifty to sixty people made up n entire Revue, and the bus driver, Stevie and I were the only ones *ever* on time. I'd been raised to be punctual. I expected the same of Stevie, but my insistence on his being prompt had to do with more than upbringing. Getting places early is an asset for a blind person. By arriving first, Stevie was able to recognize others as they arrived and learn where they were sitting.

Still, I was astounded to discover that no one else ever cared about being on time. Some, like Marvin Gaye, seemed to have absolutely no sense of time at all.

Clarence Paul laughed at my frustration. "Hey, man, you just gotta get used to CP time."

CP? What was CP? Other than Clarence's initials?

"Colored people's time," Clarence answered. "We get there, don't we? So relax."

I tried but never succeeded. Stevie and I continued to show up when we were supposed to.

Band members who operated on "CP time" drove promoters nuts. Ready and set for a show, Stevie and I would sit waiting for the musicians or the music director to arrive. The audiences fidgeted. The promoters, sure the show wouldn't go on, got angry. And I wished I were anyplace else, because they thought I should be able to do something about it.

Whenever I was in charge of setting our schedule, I'd fudge on it some to try working around the problem. If our plane was to leave at eight, I'd tell everybody it left at seven. But even that didn't always work. Gene Shelby would pick me up first, pretty much on time. We'd drive over to get Stevie, and he'd be fifteen minutes late. Then over to Clarence's, where we'd wait half an hour, then to Pistol Allen's, who *still* wasn't ready—even though by now we were nearly an hour behind schedule. Living on "CP time" made for some harrowing, hundred-mile-an-hour dashes to the airport. On those rides, I was thankful my vision kept me from clearly seeing the telephone poles whiz past or the danger we must have been to everyone else on the road.

On the stage, Motown's stars delivered glamour. Off stage, I discovered the humanness of these stars. Out front, the audience saw the costumes and the training and the act. On the bus and back stage, I saw the real people beneath the fancy trappings.

I liked everyone but had little in common with most, which kept me something of an outsider. If Esther or Beans was along, I could sometimes talk with them when they weren't busy handling management responsibilities. Occasionally the bus driver and I would hit it off, but he had to concentrate on the road. Mostly, I felt alone and lonely in the midst of the great time everyone else seemed to be having.

These were highly creative people, but few had any interest in education. Many were high school dropouts, while I was a college graduate. They were performers; I was a teacher. I was in my mid-twenties, and most of them were younger. They'd spent much of their lives in Detroit's inner city. I came from the Tennessee mountains and had lived just about everywhere in the country. I was far from well off, but compared to the lives of poverty they'd experienced, it seemed I was. I had choices. They had few. For most of them, Motown was their only shot at making their dreams come true.

A big part of Motown's success resulted from Gordy knowing the acts needed more than just musical ability. Motown couldn't afford for them to appear unsophisticated. Berry hired Maxine Powell, an elegant woman with the combined knowledge of Miss Manners, Emily Post and

Amy Vanderbilt. In a house across the street from Hitsville, she conducted etiquette classes all the Motown stars were required to attend.

The Temptations were an example of the polish Maxine and Motown's choreographer, Cholly Atkins, taught. On stage, Otis Williams, Melvin Franklin, Paul Williams and Eddie Kendricks were well dressed and handsome, exacting and precise in their movements. But every bit of it, including their speech, was scripted. Backstage, from their dressing room, all you heard was "mother" this and "mother" that.

Mary Wells' stage presence, the way she carried herself and handled her music, also was extremely sophisticated. A gorgeous young woman, her beauty was enhanced even more by Motown. The gowns chosen for her were stunning. In her act, she seemed so articulate. But it was all the illusion of the stage.

One night on our first trip with the Revue, Stevie and I were, as usual, packed up early after a show and the first back on the bus. Mary was the next person to arrive. When she came back to chat, I realized that Mary Wells the person was far from the well rehearsed star her fans knew. Mary's vocabulary was so limited and her grammar so poor that we really had difficulty carrying on a conversation.

In a way, I realized, it was like meeting a foreign singer who can perform American music perfectly. Only when you try to talk do you discover there's a language barrier that makes it impossible to communicate. Because Mary had received so little schooling and virtually no cultural exposure, she simply didn't have anything to talk about. The discovery saddened me, but reinforced my determination that Stevie would obtain a good education.

There were exceptions, whose natural intelligence and desire to improve served as both a role model for Stevie and a source of support for me in my work. It's interesting to look back and realize that those were the early Motown stars whose success continues today, like Diana Ross, Smokey Robinson and a few others.

My personal favorite was that soulful singer, Kim Weston. Then married to Mickey Stevenson, Motown's powerful director of artists and repertoire, this pretty woman always conducted herself in a ladylike manner and was always a delight to talk to.

Another lady with a lot of class and pizzazz was Gladys Knight. By the time Gladys and the Pips joined Motown, she was already very polished, but beneath the stage appearance it was apparent she was a bright and capable individual.

Traveling with the Motown Revue was nothing like touring with the Mormon Tabernacle Choir. This was a rowdy bunch and everyone aboard the bus liked to party hard. Truth is, so did I. But as Stevie's guardian, I had to set a different standard.

Cards were a regular form of diversion. Clarence, Shorty Long, Choker Campbell and others kept a continual poker game going, carrying on at the top of their lungs. (Choker was great to be around and his band was terrific. But he had to be careful in most of the towns we played. It seemed there was always a sheriff hovering around looking for him, trying to collect unpaid alimony.)

Using a pack that had been brailled, Stevie and I played games more suited to his age using a pack that had been brailled. When the guys lost their poker deck one night, Stevie lent them his cards. They appreciated it. Until they noticed the raised bumps on the cards and became suspicious that it was a marked deck. Threats started to fly, and fists nearly did before we convinced them it was only braille.

On bus trips, time got all screwed up. We'd stop only for food, fuel or to do a show, rarely with a chance to shower or get refreshed first. When the show was over, we usually climbed back on the bus and kept right on riding. I'd sleep for an hour and then be awake for an hour. With nothing else to do, out of boredom I'd sleep some more. Sleep on the bus was never restful.

On occasion we'd be lucky enough to drag our worn out selves into a hotel lobby—all fifty or more of us trying to check in at the same time. Then we had all the baggage to unload. But it still wasn't time to rest. My limited eyesight meant I had to slowly familiarize myself with the room layout, then teach Stevie to navigate it by himself. Using the edge of the bed to guide his steps, he'd learn where the night tables, lamps and telephone were. With his hand brushing the wall, I'd show him how to recognize the closet space and the door to the bathroom. Every time we stayed in a hotel, the process had to be repeated. It took months of such experiences before I was comfortable with letting Stevie stay in a room by himself.

Even with good practice, problems could develop. Like the night I awoke to use the toilet. As usual, I was sleeping in the nude. I found what I thought was the bathroom door, opened it and walked through. The second I heard it swing shut behind me I knew my mistake. I'd gone out the main door and was standing, naked as the first time my mother ever saw me, in the fifth floor hallway. After minutes of frantically attempting to open my room door, I was forced to ride the elevator down to the lobby and signal a bellboy for help. He laughed all the way back up to my floor.

After too short a rest, we'd usually have time for breakfast, then it was time to start thinking about rehearsals, getting to that night's gig, and then about traveling to the next show. It was a relentless, mind and body numbing cycle. But there was no other way to accomplish the Motown mission.

The drudgery of travel extended beyond the bus. The Revue mostly appeared at dances held in stark civic centers and auditoriums. In the early years, Motown was still considered black music, which meant we often played in the poorer part of towns with no place to go for diversion. I couldn't have taken off, though, even if I had wanted to—Stevie and I had to be backstage from the opening act until his closing appearance.

On weekends, we'd occasionally spend a few days in one city, with three or four shows scheduled each day in larger theaters. While we could count on a break from the bus and stay in a hotel each night, there was little other relief. For me, it usually came from the other acts on the bill. After hearing nothing but the same songs over and over again from the Motown groups, other performers meant a welcome change of pace.

It also meant a chance to meet different people. B.B. King was on the show with us once at the Regal Theater in Chicago. Getting to know him that week, and running into him over the course of the years was a joy—I never tired of listening to his thrilling blues. But my biggest thrill was discovering what a down-to-earth, decent and fatherly guy he was, even in his mid-30's. Black performers weren't rich, but bluesmen like B.B., who'd been hitting the R&B chart hits since the year Stevie was born, earned even less money that Motown artists—he likes to say that being a black bluesman from Mississippi was like being born black twice. Yet his love for his music made it worth the stays in seedy hotels and driving himself from gig to gig. That kind of commitment and integrity was a subtle and important lesson to Stevie whenever we worked the same shows.

Then, we'd be off to Harlem and the Apollo. Two traditional theaters back to back. All those hours backstage, with nothing to do but work on Stevie's lessons and make sure he wasn't learning things he didn't need to know. And over the years, it seemed there were always plenty of such opportunities.

Peaches, of Peaches and Herb, was the center of one incident. The soul duo wasn't a Motown act, but appeared on a bill with us in 1967 singing their hits *Close Your Eyes* and *For Your Love*. One night at the Apollo, I was hanging out in the dressing room being shared by most of the musicians. Gene Kee, our musical director, was there and knew nearly everyone from his days with the Platters. He was a great guy, someone I really enjoyed working with, and a good role model for Stevie. Usually, that is.

Peaches came into the dressing room. Gene walked up to her, put both of his hands on her breasts and said, "Hey, how you doing?"

She just smiled and said, "Why, I'm doing fine." As if this was the way a woman always expected to be greeted. I couldn't believe either of them would act that way in front of a sixteen-year-old boy.

There were a lot of occasions when things went on backstage that I didn't approve of. I often saw what looked like drug deals taking place.

And there was a time at Apollo when I noticed Ardena Johnston wearing a beautiful leather outfit. She proudly told me it was new. The next morning I heard it had been sold to her by someone fencing stolen clothing backstage. Whether Ardena knew that, I don't know.

That evening, between performances, Stevie and I were in the dressing room. The door opened and Gene Shelby, our driver, walked in. Behind him, two heads peered around the edge of the door, looked me up and down for a few seconds, then closed the door and left. Not a word had been said.

"Gene, what was that all about?" I asked.

"Oh, you just got fitted." His response was as casual as if I'd asked him the time.

"What? Whatever I got fitted for, I don't want it! What do they do, steal the stuff on special order?"

"Sure," Gene said. "It's like the joke where one guy asks the other, 'How'd you like a leather coat like the one that guy's wearing?' 'Yeah, man, I like that coat!' yells his buddy. 'Hold it down,' the first guy says, 'he's still wearing it.'"

Mostly, backstage was almost as boring for me as being on the bus. But not for Stevie. As star of the show and because he was so young, he was the darling of all the other acts. They loved playing with him and he loved learning from the other musicians. Keeping his mind on school was nearly impossible at times because of the constant parade of people through the dressing room. He got bored only when I made him concentrate on lessons or finish his homework.

Since most of the other performers were only a few years older than Stevie, they treated him like a kid brother. Whenever he could get away from me, he'd be off visiting in other dressing rooms. The Marvelettes were always cuddling, kidding and joking with him. With the Temptations, I had to be very careful. I never wanted Stevie in their dressing room but I'm sure he got in anyway. He loved being around them.

Among the Motown acts, there always seemed to be an undercurrent of competitive envy. If Martha Reeves and the Vandellas had a hit song on the charts, the Marvelettes didn't like it. If the Marvelettes were more popular, Martha would get snippy about it. But for some reason that jealousy didn't spill over to Stevie. Maybe it had to do with my trying to isolate him from such petty envies. Maybe it had to do with his age or being blind, or simply because he always was enthusiastic about everyone else's success.

It was Beans Bowles who realized from the start that what Little Stevie did best was perform live. The "hi-fi" monophonic recording methods hardly enhanced his childish, high, thin singing voice. And the incredible energy he let loose on stage couldn't be recorded at all. The energy he fed the audience was fed right back, even before his first No. 1 hit. Before long, Motown star after Motown star objected to following Stevie on stage.

At one of the very first Motown Revue shows, even before *Fingertips* was recorded, Stevie and Clarence were the opening act at Chicago's Regal Theater. The slot was his because he had no major hits at the time. Stevie did several numbers, none of which were at the top of the charts—songs like *The Masquerade Is Over*, *I Call It Pretty Music (But The Old Folks Call It The Blues)*, Ray Charles' *Hallelujah I Love Her So*, and *Tears In Vain*. But even then he whipped the audience to frenzy level. An opening act was supposed to warm up the crowd, but not get it that hot!

Berry was totally pleased with Stevie's effect on the audience, but it meant smoothing the ruffled feathers of performers following Stevie. For the second show, Berry moved Stevie back in the lineup, just before Smokey Robinson and the Miracles. Again, his effect on the audience was so strong that Smokey made it clear they wouldn't follow Stevie again. Berry then pushed Stevie into what's known as a "cold dark spot," the weakest segment of the show. He didn't dare move Stevie back to just before Mary Wells closing act, and he sure couldn't bump her out of that spot. Everyone just had to contend with their frustration over Stevie's amazing effect on audiences—and it was a situation that never changed.

Several years later, when Stevie was seventeen, we played the Toronto Civic Center. Comedian Red Buttons opened. Stevie went on next. The Supremes—Motown's biggest superstars at the time—were to finish the show. Typically, Stevie got everyone pumped and screaming.

Backstage, I watched as Diana Ross turned to Berry. "Just how are we supposed to follow *that*?"

All he could do was shake his head and tell her, "You just go out there and do what you always do."

Secretly, I was thrilled for Stevie. After the show, I told him about it, and he laughed with pride.

* * *

Other than Clarence Paul, whom Stevie adored, Smokey Robinson was without a doubt his favorite person at Motown. Smokey was very bright and highly respected by everyone, and I knew he cared about Stevie. So much that he once challenged me about a decision I made.

Lula made Stevie wear a hat. It was one of those broad-brimmed fedoras that looked sharp on a mature businessman. On teenaged Stevie, I thought it looked silly. But the choice was Lula's, not mine. What was up to me was to make sure he didn't lose it. Being a typical kid, more often than not he'd leave it wherever he put it down. Every time we got back on the bus, I'd ask, "Stevie, where's your hat?"

"Oh! I left it."

To save time, off I'd go to find the hat. Finally, I was fed up with his forgetfulness.

"I'm not going after your hat any more," I told him. "It's your hat and you're responsible for it."

"Okay. I'm not going to lose it," he promised.

Sure enough, after our next quick stop Stevie returned to the bus bear-headed. I didn't say a word. He didn't say anything either, but I knew he was thinking about it.

A few seconds later, Smokey called out, "Hey, Stevie, where's your hat?"

Stevie had to confess, "Uh, man, I left it in there."

"Hey, Ted," Smokey said, "aren't you going to get his hat?"

"Nope."

"Why, man? Why aren't you going to get his hat?"

"Because, damn it Smokey, I've done it about ten times on this tour and I told him I'm not doing it again. He's got to learn to remember his own hat."

"I don't think that's right," Smokey grumbled angrily.

"I don't care whether you think it's right or not," I answered.

Smokey turned his head away and mumbled, "Okay, man."

About half an hour later, he came up behind me and put his hand on my shoulder. "You know, Ted, you're right. I'm sorry about that. You're absolutely right."

So there were no more hat problems, because the hat was gone. And I'd gained the respect of a man I liked and knew Stevie admired.

Smokey and Stevie thought it was the funniest thing to talk to each other in made-up words. They'd picked up the idea from a stand-up comic someplace. Smokey would get on the bus and say something like, "Hey, Stevie, what about your comblumidator? I think you zerked it when you pulled that wombol."

Stevie would immediately quip back, "Oh, no, man, I'm cool. You're the one who'd better watch out for the bleffins."

We all had to find ways to entertain ourselves and each other. Traveling for up to a solid month on a Greyhound bus forced us to forge bonds as companions. But exhaustion and dreariness were my most constant companions. And when we weren't out with a Motown Revue, Stevie still had other shows to do. Rarely were we home in Detroit or at the School for the Blind for more than a few days in a row.

Love A-Go-Go

"The tours are good. The last one, they said to me, 'Man, you won't need your white cane tomorrow. The suction's going to pull you into the plane.' "

— *Stevie Wonder*

American rock stars were reeling under "the British invasion" of fabulous musicians, singers and songwriters. From the Beatles to Gerry & The Pacemakers, the "Mersey Beat" created the greatest rivalry Motown had yet to face. When Berry Gordy decided it was time to return fire, it was Stevie Wonder he sent to woo England's fans. This was a tour Stevie and I were both thrilled to make.

London, of course, provided wonderful academic opportunities. But it was Liverpool—a port city suddenly fascinating American teenagers, that really excited us. It was the Beatles' hometown, and Stevie was going to perform at the famous Cavern Club, where the Beatles got their start.

Our first morning, Stevie and I made our way down to the modest hotel restaurant. After the waiter took our breakfast orders, I outlined the day's schedule. First, school lessons. Next, a press conference. Then, finally, some free time. Always looking to turn travel into learning, I suggested we could visit the famous port, from where the Titanic had sailed, or the Maritime Museum.

The waiter served our breakfast. As Stevie poured milk on his cereal, he asked, "Can I have the sugar?"

"'Pass the sugar, please,'" I automatically corrected. I handed him the small bowl at my left. He spooned the white crystals over his cereal.

When he took his first bite, I noticed Stevie suddenly seemed a bit strange. "Is everything all right?"

"Mm-hmm. Want the sugar?" He held the small bowl out to me.

I liberally sprinkled its contents over my cereal and lifted a spoonful to my lips. As soon as it hit my tongue, the cereal and sputtering gags both erupted from my mouth. The only thing louder than my choking was Stevie's laughter.

The waiter rushed to my side, certain, I'm sure, I was dying. When I was able to speak, all I could say was, "Salt. Not sugar!"

"Why, of course, sir," the waiter responded. He picked up a small bowl I hand' seen. "This is the sugar bowl. That's the salt cellar, sir."

By now, Stevie was laughing so hard he could barely breathe. Always quick to take advantage of an opportunity for a good practical joke, he'd endured his own mouthful of salty cereal to get me. And he'd got me good.

The visit to Liverpool ended on a much tastier note. With one of the many talented local bands, Stevie performed at The Cavern Club, where John, Paul, George and Ringo first gained fame. Its name accurately described the place. A series of small rooms carved from the underground rock, there was no ventilation, no heat, no air conditioning and, seemingly, no limit to the number of people allowed to jam themselves in. But the sound that reverberated off those ancient stone walls was incredible. Imagine the best rock performance you've ever attended being held in a tiled bathroom, and you'll have a slight idea of the pulsing, mesmerizing action felt by everyone in the place.

None of the Beatles was on hand for Stevie's show at the Cavern, but Paul McCartney came to a show we did in London. After the final set, Stevie, Paul, Clarence and I sat around acting like a proverbial mutual admiration society—Paul going on and on about how the Beatles loved rhythm and blues and how they all admired Stevie's music and the Motown sound; the rest of us quizzing him about the "Fab Four." It was the only time in all my years of working alongside the greatest singers and musicians in the world that I ever asked for an autograph, which earned me major points with my sisters Joan and Diane. And that chance meeting was the start of the musical friendship between Paul and Stevie that, nearly twenty years later, led to their No. 1 hit *Ebony & Ivory*.

The whole trip to England was exhilarating, and was made more memorable by my first experience with an exceptionally unprincipled promoter. Over the years, Stevie and I became proficient at catching on to less than honest tactics. In London, it took us a while to realize we were dealing with the sort of smarmy fellow who'd pat you on the back with one hand and pick your pocket with the other.

"While you're here I want to make sure everything goes just fine," the promoter promised. "If there's anything I can do for you, just say the word. If you need a car and driver, let me know. They're yours."

I gladly took him up on that generous offer. We took field trips all over London and Stevie learned a lot. My lesson came later. At the end of the tour, five hundred dollars was deducted from Stevie's fee, for use of the car and driver.

The promoter also told me I could "use" his pretty, blonde secretary for the weekend. Naively, I thought he'd meant as secretarial help. Once I saw the charge for the car, it dawned on me he meant something much different, and could just imagine what that would have cost! To top it off, he "forgot" to reimburse us for certain expenses and "lost" some of our equipment.

I should have seen the warning signs on our first visit to his office. Al-though we had an appointment, we were kept waiting nearly an hour. The only seating in the reception room was a sloped bench attached to the wall. We didn't so much sit as brace ourselves on it. After this uncomfortable detainment, Stevie, Clarence and I were ushered into the Great Promoter's presence. His office had to be at least thirty feet long. Near the door were the visitors' chairs. Far, far away, at the opposite end of the room, was his desk. We practically had to yell at each other in order to be heard.

He proudly told us how, when he decided to go into the booking business, he decided to do things "exactly like they did it in America." Never before or after did I meet any promoter who handled business like this character. Promoters have a well earned reputation for doing whatever they can to increase their profits, but they know the bottom line is to keep the clubs and audiences happy. Which meant things like getting the act to the show on time.

Not this fellow. Before one show, we'd been ready on time, as usual. But the driver wasn't. We didn't arrive at the club until long after Stevie was to have performed. The club was packed with a fidgeting crowd and the owner greeted us through clenched teeth. But after the long delay and drive, Stevie really needed to take care of something before going on stage.

"Stevie needs to use the bathroom first," I told the owner.

The man exploded with a volley of expletives. "I can't believe this! You're forty-five minutes late! And now he wants to take a *bath*!"

Ah, yes, I remembered—just because we both spoke English didn't mean we spoke the same language. I'd completely forgotten that to the British, a toilet was called a water closet. Once we cleared up that misunderstanding, Stevie was on stage in a matter of minutes. Typically, he won the crowd over, even though two members of the house band were so whacked on booze and drugs that they could barely perform.

Our driver wasn't much better. It was his job to wait during Stevie's performances and drive us back to the hotel. What we didn't know was that he spent his time drinking. One night he scared the bejeesus out of us by driving over sidewalks and everywhere but on the road. Clarence and I had to bodily stop him and the car and then find another way to get Stevie and ourselves back to the hotel.

* * *

Other Motown stars had made individual trips to England. In the spring of 1966, Berry decided the time was right to send a Motown Revue. Hot off the road from other shows, Stevie and I winged across the Atlantic, this time with the Temptations, Martha and the Vandellas, the Supremes, Smokey and the Miracles, plus Berry, Esther and Beans. Landing at Heathrow Airport, hundreds of fans greeted us with signs proclaiming Motown Appreciation Day. We did appreciate it, and every one of us now knew the thrill the Beatles must have felt when they first arrived in New York City.

Ed Sullivan had been responsible for getting thousands of teens to show up when John, Paul, George and Ringo first landed in America. Gordy and another fellow were the ones who orchestrated our London turnout. On the surface, it gave Motown more popularity than we actually had there at the time.

Getting someone famous on the British music scene to travel with the Revue was important for us to draw crowds and be a success. Truthfully, Berry had trouble finding an English recording star willing to join the tour. Finally he recruited Georgie Fame. Georgie's big British hit at that time was *Yeh, Yeh*, but he didn't break into the American Top 10 until 1968 with *The Ballad of Bonnie & Clyde*. His jazzy pop songs were totally unlike the Motown sound, but we needed any help we could get to attract audiences.

In just about every way, it was a normal Motown Revue. We performed two shows nightly for twenty out of the twenty-four days, traveling by bus. We quickly realized that the highways back home were a breeze compared to the grueling effort of getting around England. With no expressways, even a hundred-mile trip could take the better part of a day. Food, when we could find it along the route, was less than mediocre. Although the bus didn't break down, it rode terribly rough and was unbelievably noisy. The air brake release valve was inside, so every time the driver hit the brakes an enormous hiss drowned out all conversation. Getting any sleep or doing any of Stevie's school work was virtually impossible.

Still, new fans and new experiences kept things lively. Although, at one point in Wales, we had an experience so lively it nearly gave us all heart attacks.

The morning after our show in Cardiff, we climbed back aboard the bus. Stevie and I sat about three rows from the door. The usual commotion ensued as everyone settled in for the long ride. We'd been underway only moments when the driver suddenly slammed on the brakes. A masked gunman burst through the doors. Behind him were four others.

It's amazing how fast pandemonium can erupt, and how fast your mind works in panic. Stevie couldn't see what was going on and I was too stunned to tell him. All I could imagine was the headlines back home: "Motown Stars Robbed, Murdered in Wales."

Instead, the robbers whipped off their masks. The uproar turned to roars of laughter. We'd just been "held up" by the Temptations. Aided by the British emcee traveling with us—who'd generously supplied the toy guns—and abetted by our driver, none of us had noticed that Otis Williams, Melvin Franklin, David Ruffin, Paul Williams and Eddie Kendricks hadn't gotten on the bus at the hotel.

The Tempts never failed to puzzle me. Their stage sophistication was the exact opposite of their off-stage drinking, cursing and carousing. And the way they actually acted was often in direct contrast to statements they made. One day a bunch of us were sitting around talking about how life on the road was lonely, especially for the married guys. One of the Tempts got to talking about his wife. He went on and on about how much he loved her, how much he missed her. He told us about all the things they'd do when he got home. He talked about all the plans they had for the future. He was holding a newspaper and the more he talked, the more melancholy he became, the tighter and tighter he rolled that paper.

Finally, he stood and snapped the newspaper under his arm. Clarence asked, "Where you going?"

"I can't take it no more," he answered. "I'm gonna go find me a woman."

Since he was a lot less despondent when I saw him next, I guess he did just that.

Egos always affect people working together, and in the music industry big egos are the rule, not the exception. I simply ignored them unless Stevie or I were directly affected. Sometimes it was Stevie's own ego that needed a bit of reigning in. At the Cardiff show, the band did a terrible job with his music. By the end of his final number, Stevie was livid. He stormed off stage without so much as a nod to the applauding audience.

Beans approached him calmly. "Stevie, don't you think you out to go out there and take a little bow?"

Stevie refused. It was obvious he was so mad he didn't want to listen to anyone.

"You know," Beans continued quietly, "you're only hurting yourself if you don't."

Stevie thought about it for a second. "Yeah, I know. It's not them I'm mad at. I'm sorry." He took my arm and I led him back on stage where he graciously thanked his newest fans.

In the cramped confines of the bus, everyone made a special effort to put egos aside and try hard to get along. Except for one person. Martha Reeves was as temperamental, to put it politely, as she was talented. Also, she was the only one in Motown who consistently let me know she did not like me expressly because I was white. Naturally, I never felt comfortable around her and just tried to steer clear of her. But on tours, no one escaped the tension Martha created.

In her book, *Dancing in the Street*, she says an incident in 1967— refusing to sing a particular song line in *I Can't Dance To That Music You're Playing*, gave her the reputation at Motown of "being difficult to work with." That may be, but Martha had always been difficult to travel with. Only when I read her book did I learn of the difficulties she faced over those years. Maybe if we'd known what kind of troubles she had, all of us would have been more understanding. But we didn't. All we could do was try to keep our distance from her temperamental, distrustful nature.

During the Revue in England when we had a couple days' break in the show schedule, I saw a chance to take Stevie on an excursion. Next thing I knew, Martha was coming along. So was Van Sauter, a reporter from the *Detroit Free Press* who was covering part of our tour.

The two days traveling through the gorgeous English countryside turned out to be more pleasant than I'd anticipated, though I never relaxed to the point of having fun. The trains we rode carried few other passengers. No one recognized either Martha or Stevie, which gave us all a much appreciated break from business. Van was bright and personable, full of both interesting stories and questions about Stevie's education. Stevie was as chatty and curious as always. He never had any trouble talking with Martha but she barely spoke to either Van or me.

(In just those couple of days I began to feel a real friendship develop with Van, who soon headed back to Detroit and on to assignment in Vietnam. After our tour, I wrote him at the Caravelle Hotel where the press stayed in Saigon. Within days, the news came that the hotel had been bombed, killing several people. When my letter eventually came back marked "undeliverable," I assumed the worst. I often thought of how Van's company had made our time on the train enjoyable for me, and thought it was such a shame what happened. It was more than thirty years before I learned that Van hadn't been killed in that bomb attack. Instead, he'd gone on to become president of CBS television news programming and other successful ventures.)

Only once can I recall Martha being fun to be around during that entire tour. The year before, Dusty Springfield had played in the States and she and Martha became friends. The whole Motown group was staying at London's Cumberland Hotel, one of those posh places where, if shoes are left outside your door at night, a valet picks them up, polishes them and returns them before morning. Dusty, Martha, Stevie and I came back together late one night and Dusty had us all in high spirits. As we left the elevator at our floor, she and Martha lagged behind, giggling. When Stevie and I stopped at our rooms, the two women were scurrying up and down the hall, switching all the shoes around. Somehow, I doubt the other guests thought the joke was quite as funny as we did.

*   *   *

Traveling was always exhausting, but this tour pushed me to the limit. To promote Motown, as many publicity appearances as possible were scheduled for everyone. Gordy also was trying to establish a British label for the company, which meant we were expected to meet and greet a lot of recording executives. Between performances, bus trips, promotional appearances, press conferences, and radio station visits, every minute was filled. It all compounded my already extensive duties as Stevie's teacher—fitting in classes and field trips in when I could, plus being road manager, valet and chaperone. My fatigue became overwhelming.

Adding to the difficulty was that my only eye had started giving me trouble just before we left on the tour. Stevie and Kim Weston were both appearing on *The Steve Allen Show* out in Hollywood. The morning of the show, before leaving for the television studio, I'd noticed a silvery gray flickering mass about the size of a dime in the center of my vision. What was worrisome was that I couldn't see through it.

As Stevie and I sat in the audience before his appearance, a lady sat down beside me and said brightly, "Say, I know you."

I was embarrassed, because I couldn't recognize who it was. When I looked at her, all I could see was this flickering dead spot. I stammered and stuttered around until I realized, from her voice, that it was Kim.

My eyesight continued to worsen and it became even more difficult for me to see in poorly lit situations, such as back stage or walking the narrow streets of England at night. With no vision in my right eye, the condition in my left eye was adding to all my other feelings of frustration.

I had always impressed upon Stevie that tiredness and frustration were no excuse for shirking responsibilities, taking irritation out on others, or illegal drug use. Unfortunately, in England I failed to keep one of my own rules and nearly broke another.

While in London, I had a business appointment but wasn't sure how I'd reach my destination. One of the guys working for the promoter heard I needed transportation. "We've an extra seat in our car," he offered. "We'll take you."

I crowded aboard with a couple fellows from the promoter's crew and another couple who worked for Dusty. Several conversations were going at once when, seemingly out of nowhere, a huge truck pulled directly into our path. It struck us broadside. The impact sent us slamming into each other as the little English auto was nearly cut in two.

Once we got out and saw how much damage the car had sustained, it was astounding we hadn't all been killed. None of us was even bleeding. The bobbies who arrived repeatedly urged us to go to the hospital. On tight schedules, we each refused.

*Little Stevie Wonder's first
photo card for his fans.*

*Stevie's second photo card—with
a plug for Hohner Harmonicas.*

At home with his brothers, sister and mother Lula Mae,
Stevie was just another kid.

Even on the plane, Stevie continued experimenting with his music.

Clarence Paul teamed up with Stevie to sing Bob Dylan's Blowin' In the Wind.

Motown's studio musicians, "The Funk Brothers,"
backed Stevie and all the other great Motown artists.

The Lincoln Memorial and the world became Stevie's classroom when we traveled.

One human and many feathered fans joined me, Stevie and Beau Bohannon (far right) in London's Trafalgar Square

In class at the Michigan School for the Blind, Stevie studied his assignments in braille.

Stevie hosting a jam session at the Michigan School for the Blind.

On a night flight to a show, Stevie got a lesson at the controls.

Reading braille music, Stevie practiced a lesson at the piano where he later wrote My Cherie Amour.

Dr. Robert Thompson, superintendent at the Michigan School for the Blind.

Former state representative George Edwards, Esther's husband, presented a proclamation from the Michigan State Legislature to Stevie during graduation ceremonies at the School for the Blind.

Stevie was the only one to catch a fish on our deep-sea fishing trip, and he was asleep at the time.

Stevie posed near the Apollo Theater for an album cover.

In Tokyo, Stevie and I (far l) visited with students at the Japan Education University High School of the Blind.

Stevie and the Motor Town Revue enjoyed traditional dining in Japan.

A special ceremony was held for Stevie at a notable tea ceremony school in Tokyo. Standing with her students, in the dark kimono, was Mrs. Sogetsu Shimada, one of Japan's three leading tea ceremony masters. Kneeling, (l-r), were Mr. Shimada, me; Stevie; Don Hunter; and Gene Shelby.

Stevie's mother Lula, an unidentified nun,
Stevie, Esther, Mrs. Hubert Humphrey and
I, (l-r) at a ceremony in Washington, D.C.

Stevie, his mother and Junious Griffin
met President Richard M. Nixon in the
White House Rose Garden in 1969.

On a return visit to campus in 1988, Stevie
visited with two of his favorite teachers,
Lucy Karner (l) and Ginny Wiehn (r).

On that same visit, Dr. Thompson (third from left) and staff
from the Michigan School for the Blind posed with Stevie.

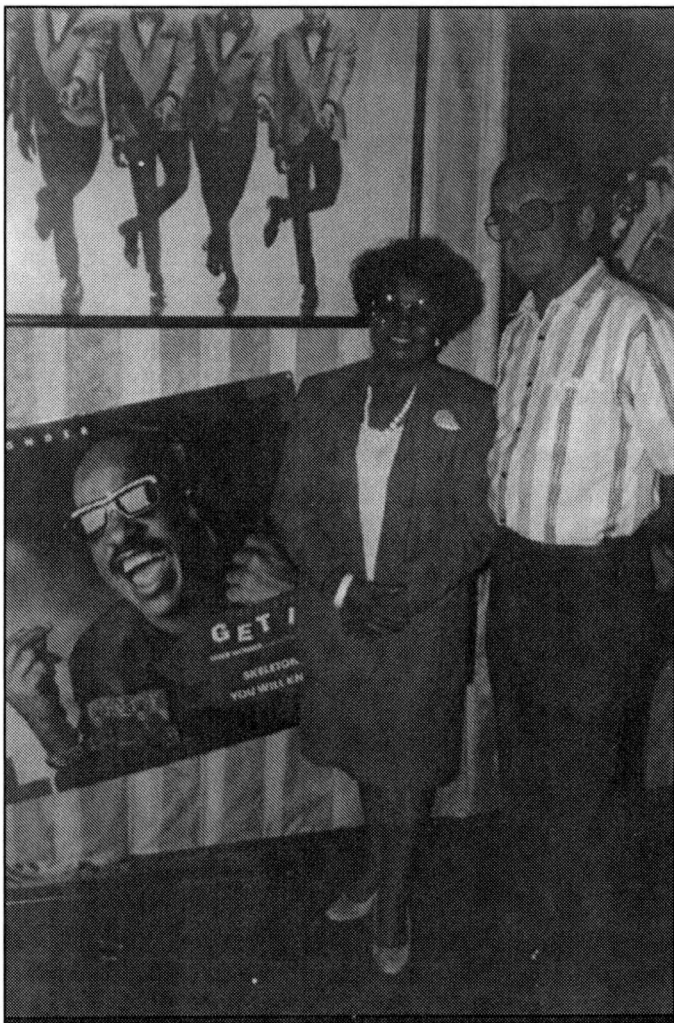

Esther Gordy Edwards—as lovely as ever—
with me at the Motown Historical Museum in 1995.

ITINERARY—STEVIE WONDER
JUNE 7-JUNE 24, 1967

June 7   Leave Detroit 8:15 a.m. on United 477. Arrive Chicago 9:14 a.m.
          Leave Chicago 10:00 a.m. on United 143. Arrive Seattle 12 noon.
          Leave Seattle 1:45 p.m. on United 298. Arrive Vancouver 2:19 p.m.

          1 sedan and 1 wagon in Ted Hull's name at Hertz.

          8 singles reserved at Georgian Towers, 1450 W. Georgia St. 604-
          MU. 1-4321

Engagement   Isy's Supper Club (June 7-17)

Rehearsal   3:30 p.m.

June 19   Leave Vancouver 10:10 a.m. on United 849. Arrive Seattle 10:57
          a.m. Leave Seattle 11:55 a.m. on United 144. Arrive Chicago 5:25
          p.m. (Stevie and Gene Shelby have seats reserved on American 706
          leaving Chicago 6:25 p.m. Arrive Detroit 7:26 p.m. Return to
          Chicago on American 509 6:00 p.m. Arrive Chicago 701 p.m. on the
          19th if needed.

          1 sedan and 1 wagon at Hertz in Ted Hull's name.

          Hotel accommodations will be called to you in Vancouver.

Engagement   Whiskey A Go Go (June 19-29)

Rehearsal   3:00 p.m.

June 30   Open return

          **Note: Gene Xee and Stevie will leave Chicago on June 24th at 8:10
          a.m. on American 354. Arrive Detroit at 9:01 a.m. for the Fox Theatre
          gig.

          After gig: Leave Detroit 7:35 p.m. on Northwest 231. Arrive Chicago
          8:30 p.m.

*My absence from most of this itinerary was due to the fact I took a few days off to
return home to Detroit long enough to get married!*

I was thankful Stevie wasn't with me and grateful to be alive. But in my utter exhaustion, all I felt was building anger over the pressures I was under. After keeping my appointment, as I headed back to the theater, I seethed over the unrelenting pace, and having to go directly from shows in the States to the British tour with no break in between. I was exhausted by the relentless travel and the obligations heaped on me.

I allowed myself to descend into a pity party, focusing on all that seemed wrong in my life. I was sick of feeling used and not getting one red cent for all the extra work. I was the one who had to make sure Stevie's stage uniforms were cleaned and pressed between bus trips and show time. I had to maintain his school equipment working, and just a couple days earlier the talking book machine broke. I was in charge of all his expenses and had to account for every single penny. I was with a teenager twenty-four-hours a day with no time to myself. By the time I returned backstage, I was so mad I didn't want to speak to anyone.

Word of the auto accident quickly spread through the crew. Esther rushed to find me, fluttering with motherly concern. I refused to believe it was sincere. In my mind, neither she nor Gordy nor anyone at Motown gave a hoot about anything except the income I or anyone else represented. I snarled at her like an angry dog. Esther's eyes widened in hurt surprise. Without a word, she rushed from the room.

The close friendship we'd enjoyed became cautious and distant for a time after that. I apologized and blamed my worn-out state for my lousy temper. I knew Esther didn't have an insincere bone in her body and truly was worried about me. It took some time to admit I'd been wrong to think otherwise. it took even longer to realize I really should have had medical attention after the auto accident. It's probable I'd sustained a concussion in the collision, which would have led to behavior so out of character for me. Instead, I'd blamed everyone and everything else.

An attorney was part of our extended entourage in England. "Boy, you really look tired," he commented a few days after the auto accident.

"No kidding. I hadn't noticed," I felt like snapping. Managing to control the impulse, I simply agreed with him.

As nonchalantly as if he were offering an aspirin, he asked, "You want some uppers?"

Casual drug use was just beginning to occur in the mid-'60s, but had long been a part of life for musicians. When I joined Motown, I quickly got over my surprise that many of the musicians used drugs, especially marijuana. What did surprise me was having an attorney offer me speed.

I knew the drug's lure, because I'd enjoyed its benefits before. But now the potential ramifications were too great to chance. Berry and Esther were aware some people in Motown used drugs but absolutely did not condone it. I ignored the drug use I saw unless it somehow affected me or Stevie, and on a couple of occasions did report it to Esther.

If a doctor had made the offer, I'd probably have accepted. Amphetamines had gotten me through a lot of rough times during college. Then, it had been under a doctor's care. With my visual handicap, the effort required to complete my courses was physically draining. My doctor thought possibly the cause was psychological and prescribed a mild pep pill.

Taking amphetamines under prescription was one thing, but using illicit drugs was just too far outside of my standards. I knew full well that what I did would affect Stevie. If I used illegal drugs, how could I ever expect to steer him away from them? There was nothing to do but muddle through my fatigue as best I could and survive the rest of the trip. Blessedly, the twenty-four day tour that felt like twenty-four years ended, and we headed home to Detroit.

I finally did get medical attention when we returned to the States. By then, my sight had deteriorated to the point where I had to turn my head sideways to see anything in front of me. The diagnosis was a detached retina, and I was one of the first people to undergo laser surgery to repair it, at the MacMillan Clinic in St. Louis.

For six weeks after the operation, I was forced to lay perfectly still and flat on my back. While it was a break from the road, the recuperation period was stressful instead of relaxing. I had little to do except worry about paying the hospital. Motown offered no health benefits. I'd gone through all the money I'd saved and my parents were footing the rest of the bill.

Still, after a month in the hospital, I wrote Esther and told her that if she wanted to take me off the payroll, I'd understand. I knew my salary came from Stevie's income and that now someone else had to be to look after him. Unfortunately, she took me up on the offer.

When I did return to Motown, I insisted on health insurance and, to his great credit, Berry obtained coverage for everyone within a month.

During my hospitalization, I only heard from on person at Motown. Esther, with typical humor, sent a card and note that read "I hope you get well soon and can come on back to work. Everything is just like you left it, a complete disaster!" I got a kick out of that, but I really felt forgotten by all the people I lived and worked so closely with.

*   *   *

England may have been way across the ocean, but just across the Detroit River sat its province Canada. The Motor City and Ontario were connected by the Ambassador Bridge, the Detroit-Windsor Tunnel—and music. One of the region's most influential radio stations was Windsor's CKLW, 800 on the AM dial. When the skies were right, the 50,000 watt station could be heard as far away as the Eastern Seaboard and as far south as the Carolinas. CK, as it was known, broke numerous Motown hits and made stars of every Motown artist throughout Canada. It was considered so important a radio station that Stevie had no qualms about making an exception to one of his own rules about performing.

The winter before I became his teacher, he had a date to play a dance at a Buffalo, New York, roller-rink. Buffalo is notorious for its snow storms and Stevie and Esther landed in the middle of one. Even in the miserable weather, nearly a thousand teens showed up. Unfortunately, the band didn't. They were stranded in the snow, which left "Little Stevie Wonder" stranded on stage.

Esther and the promoter were in a near panic trying to figure out how to save the show. Somebody found a small record player. Esther provided two or three of Stevie's records and told him he was going to have to pantomime the songs. In what he told me was the most humiliating performance of his life, Stevie lip synched to tunes blaring from the cheap record player's single, tiny speaker. The night was such a fiasco that the promoter gave refunds to everyone who'd shown up. Stevie told me he'd never lip synch again.

But lip synching is just part of the smoke and mirrors of performing. For movies or television shows such as Dick Clark's *American Bandstand*, it was far too expensive to stage live acts—even the musicians pantomimed to a pre-recorded sound track. On *The Ed Sullivan Show*, the singers performed live, but again, the music behind them was almost always prerecorded.

Only under such excellent conditions would Stevie agree to lip synch. One of the few places he felt especially comfortable doing so was at the record hops hosted by CKLW DJ's Dave Shafer and Tom Shannon. In professionally handled situations like those, top of the line equipment meant sound quality as good as a live performance. Stevie never had to worry about disappointing fans the station drew for him.

Radio, especially "CK" and Detroit's "Keener 13" and WJLB—home of Martha Jean, "The Queen," Steinberg, had a lot to do with Stevie becoming popular in Canada. It was in Toronto where Diana Ross questioned how the Supremes could follow him on stage. But it was in Montreal where Stevie came up against the only act he had trouble following.

A three-act variety show was set for the Macombo Club in Montreal. The first act was a locally popular group of jugglers. Next came Mugsy, a chimpanzee who had somehow achieved nationwide fame in Canada. I'll admit he was as skilled as any performer who'd ever clawed his way to the top. On stage, he stole the show every single night with antics that absolutely delighted the audience.

Backstage, Mugsy wasn't so cute. He took great pleasure in pinching people. He was the most ill-tempered creature anyone could cross paths with. The audience didn't know that though, and by the time he finished his act it was almost impossible for Stevie to get the audience's attention.

It didn't help that the crowds were older and preferred smoother, standard numbers to rock. Adding to the problem was the three-man house band, which did a lousy job with Stevie's music. Clarence Paul worked hard with them but it didn't help much. As far as the club owner was concerned, the problem wasn't his band, it was Stevie. Within days he threatened, "Either you get this show together or I'm not paying you."

Immediately, I called Beans Bowles back at the office in Detroit for help. Clarence quickly taught Stevie a couple of new numbers he thought the audience might warm up to. That evening, Benny Benjamin and Mike Terry, another Motown studio musician, were on stage. Backed by Benny's phenomenal drums and Mike's wailing baritone sax, Stevie immediately knocked any thoughts of Mugsy from the audience's mind. For the rest of the run, one of his most popular numbers was the arrangement of *Hello, Dolly* Clarence put together for him. I was really impressed that even as a fifteen-year-old, Stevie had the class and sophistication to carry off such Broadway show tunes.

A year or two later we were in Montreal again, just after Expo '67 ended. The city was still filled with tourists. Lodging was hard to find, but at the last minute Motown managed to book us near the world's fairground where Stevie would play. The weather was wet and dreary and we were glad to get out of the rain when we arrived at the very nice hotel. After registering, a bellhop came to escort us to our rooms. Stevie took my arm and we set off behind the young man.

We walked down a long hallway and turned right. We walked another long hallway and turned left. We reached a door and the bellhop opened it for us. We were back outside in the drizzling rain.

The bellhop led us along the hotel wall to the sidewalk. We turned left. We reached an intersection and waited for the light to change. We kept walking and walking. The bellhop hadn't said a single word.

By this time, I was thoroughly confused and began to wonder what kind of fishy situation we were getting into. Stevie was as perplexed, too. "I don't understand this," he whispered. "I thought the bellhop was taking us to our rooms."

He was. Only it was in an annex the hotel had acquired to help meet the huge demand created by Expo '67. The hotel itself, now more than three blocks behind us, was a fine establishment. The annex wasn't. It was a real dump, reminding me of the sleazy lodging bums found off 12th Street in downtown Detroit. No room service. No pool. No amenities. But at least no fleas.

The company always tried to put us into decent hotels, but making arrangements by phone made it difficult to tell what kind of a place we'd end up in. If Berry was along, though, we could certainly count on classy digs. For hosting business meetings and entertainment, he was especially particular about the surroundings. Even then, Stevie and I had little time to enjoy any available amenities.

Berry, his aide Don Hunter, Diana Ross and the Supremes, plus Stevie and I were staying in one such posh place in Toronto when my phone rang one day.

Don was on the line. "Hey, we're all at the pool. You and Stevie come on down."

I didn't particularly like Don. What I especially didn't like was the way he made demands, not requests. He was an example of the cliché, "It's not what you say, it's how you say it." But Berry liked an aggressive style in the people working close with him, and Don certainly had one.

"We're in the middle of school work," I told him. "This isn't a good time."

"Come on, man. Make an exception."

I'd learned years earlier that everyone thought I should "make an exception" when Motown wanted Stevie's schooling interrupted. "No, Don. I can't."

I hung up. About ten minutes later, the phone rang again. This time it was Berry.

"Hey, Ted, come on down, man." Berry's charm had a lot to do with his success and it was flowing freely now. "You guys have been working awfully hard. Just come down for just a few minutes. Let's just relax a little bit."

Well, there are times to say no to the company president, and I knew this wasn't one of them. Stevie and I headed off to the pool.

But even when he was "relaxing," Berry never stopped working. Motown was rapidly expanding its administrative staff and, in searching for ways to find quality people, he was reviewing personnel tests designed to identify capabilities. Diana Ross was reading through some of them and began quizzing us from one of the tests.

I started to worry. I'd always had trouble with tests on abstract reasoning. Usually I was pretty quick at thinking on my feet, but those things just stopped me cold. As Diana read some of the questions aloud, I couldn't even begin to pick the correct answers from the multiple choices.

I was always careful about what kind of situations I put myself in. As Stevie's teacher, I wanted to at least *appear* intelligent. I flashed back to the only time I'd been so close to being caught in such a tight spot. I'd been a student teacher when a group of observers from Michigan State University sat in on my class one day. My ten blind and visually impaired students were taking turns reading braille aloud. The last boy to read struggled with a word he didn't know how to pronounce. I looked at it and I couldn't pronounce it either. At times like that, homework is a teacher's saving grace.

"Okay," I said, praying the observers wouldn't see through me. "Let's pick up here tomorrow and see who knows what the word is."

Now, all I could do was stay silent and hope Diana would get back in the pool.

"Stevie," Diana said, "here's a good one. Let's see if you can get this. 'Your shoulder is to your body and arm' as which of the following—'a tree to the ground, a creek to its bank, a road to a hill, or a nut to its shell.' "

"Oh, shoot," I thought, completely stumped. "If he doesn't get it, they'll expect me to know the answer."

After some thought, Stevie answered, "A tree to the ground." That sounded plausible to me. Wrong.

"A creek to its bank," Diana read. "Because they meet."

That made absolutely no sense to me whatsoever. It still doesn't. I was just glad I'd become Stevie's teacher long before Berry would have expected me to pass an aptitude test.

Down To Earth

*"My proudest moment will be if I can live my life in a way
to ultimately, when I'm called, I can meet the King of All."*
                                                    —*Stevie Wonder*

"Everybody thinks they're responsible," said Don Davis, a Motown musician and producer. "The writers say 'It was the song.' The producers think 'It was the way I produced it.' The musicians think 'We did it.' The personal managers think they're responsible. The sales guys say, 'Hey, if we didn't sell the product...' And the artist thinks he or she is responsible."

When Don Davis said that, he overlooked a group I thought very important to Motown's success—promoters.

They were the people who really took the risks financially. Motown publicized its shows, but rarely acted the role of promoter. Even on Revues, it was a promoter who put his money on the line. And it was interesting that promoters weren't everywhere, which meant there were a lot of larger cities around the country we never played.

Promoters often were difficult to work with because of the tremendous monetary pressure they faced. They were essentially gamblers who said, "It'll cost me $10,000 to bring Stevie Wonder in, but I can clear $15,000 profit." The payoff could be that great if everything went right, but it took hard cash up front. Promoters were required to advance us half of Stevie's fee, plus they paid rent on the club or auditorium, arranged for security, advertising, insurance and myriad other costs. Advance ticket sales brought in only a small portion of the money they hoped to make. Ticket sales at the door delivered the lion's share of the cash, but they were the biggest uncertainty. The entire investment could be lost if something like a sudden storm kept people away.

Sometimes a promoter's financial problems became ours. The World Famous Trip Lounge in Los Angeles, which was anything but world famous, went bankrupt after our show there. There were good crowds and Stevie had nothing to do with the club's failure. It was just something that had been building over time.

After Stevie's last performance, the club owner came over. "Mr. Hull, we've got a problem. I can either pay Stevie or I can pay the musicians. The musicians really need the money. Does Stevie need it that bad? What should I do?"

Stevie's big song at the time was *For Once In My Life*. And for once in my life, I knew what had to be done. If word got around that our band hadn't been paid, we'd have a hard time hiring musicians for future gigs. "Pay the musicians," I said.

There was no question in my mind that Stevie needed his money as much as anyone. He wasn't exactly earning a fortune at that time, and Motown hadn't pushed to get him a big hit song for a couple of years. I knew the incredible workload everyone in the company had to deal with, and that the performers with the top hits got top attention. Although the company obviously cared about Stevie and all of its performers, it was often the person traveling with the act who had to make crucial decisions affecting the artist's career.

Another such occasion was in Virginia, where a promoter hired Stevie for two nightclub performances in Richmond and Virginia Beach. Stevie was about fifteen and, as a minor, not allowed to work anywhere liquor was served, but Virginia laws prohibited alcohol sales in clubs. Stevie hadn't had a decent hit since *Fingertips* and was getting few bookings at the time. Motown agreed to the two shows and gave the promoter a bargain rate.

Surprised by the low price, the promoter questioned me about it.

"Oh, Stevie just happens to have a couple dates free in the area," I said. "Ordinarily, his rate is almost twice as much as you're getting him for."

I wasn't about to admit Stevie's career was in a slump, that no one at Motown seemed able to change that, or that we were almost begging for performance dates at the time.

Stevie's evening show in Richmond went well and drew a good crowd. The next day we headed for Virginia Beach for an appearance at a casual vacation place. I don't particularly remember Stevie's performance there, but I do remember being treated to one of the silliest situations I ever encountered.

Local alcohol laws didn't stop patrons from bringing their own bottles of booze, which they politely set on the floor. Just before nine that night, every glass was whisked from the table tops and stashed with the bottles. At nine o'clock sharp, the sheriff walked in. Keeping his line of sight only on the people's heads, he slowly scanned the room. Without even a glance toward the floor, he turned and left, his legal obligation to check for liquor fulfilled. Out came the glasses and the party resumed.

Even though the crowd was large and had a good time, the owner still lost money on the show. More easy-going and philosophical than most promoters we worked with, he just shrugged and said, "Damn, I didn't have to come all the way up here to lose money. I can stay in Richmond and do that."

* * *

Management became an increasing, if unplanned, role for me partly because Stevie was too young and inexperienced to make many of the on-the-spot decisions that always surfaced for performers. The business side of management includes a million details—finding and selecting the right opportunities, which gigs to play and which ones to pass up, negotiating contracts, deciding who'll go along on the road, scheduling transportation and more. On the personal side, for me at least, it meant being a buffer between Stevie and his family as well as his liaison to Motown and Motown's International Talent Management Company, the booking division Esther directed.

Motown was no different than any other corporation—its product just happened to be performers and entertainment instead of TV sets or automobiles. Yet Esther knew that if a manager cared about the person's success, happiness and family, and worked to strengthen those important aspects of life, then both the artist and the company would profit. I saw her as more attuned to the person and his or her needs than her brother, but they both understood that keeping the artists healthy and whole was simply good business.

"Most of our artists were from one-parent and no-parent families," Esther reminded me. "And, basically, we were going to take care of them, make them into good human beings, good American citizens."

That's exactly what we did for Stevie. I was part of Motown because the Gordy's cared enough about him to hire me. But such individual attention wasn't possible for everyone else at Motown. This was a recording company, not a rehabilitation clinic. Although they couldn't control every aspect of these young adults' lives, the Gordy's did what they could to encourage individual self-improvement.

Motown's concern for its artists is proven by the fact that so many of them are still famous today—like Stevie, Diana Ross, Smokey Robinson, the Temptations, the Four Tops and Gladys Knight, to name just a few. I think Motown recognized the symbiotic nature of the business: the performers' ability to generate revenues allowed the company to continue supporting and promoting them, which meant the performers could keep earning, and so would Motown.

I learned more from Esther than from than anyone else at Motown because I worked so closely with her. I watched her deal with promoters and reporters, scheduling interviews and handling public relations. I paid close attention to how she handled people and situations. I often heard Esther say, "If you're right, you fight." But she also knew when not to.

Anyone from Detroit knew about union clout—the Teamsters and the United Auto Workers virtually ruled the area work force. What most people don't know is musicians were unionized three years before the Teamsters and nearly forty years before the UAW. The American Federation of Musicians held a power and control that reached onto every stage in the nation.

The AFM did a lot of good for musicians, but each Local's "business representative" could to stop any show without warning. These men carried a lot of weight and among performers were as revered and reviled as the Teamsters' Jimmy Hoffa or Walter Reuther of the UAW.

As we arrived to do a show in a Philadelphia club once, Clarence Paul was stopped by the rep from AFM Local #77. Stevie's union card had expired, the man claimed, and local dues were owed, too.

"Either Stevie pays up now," he insisted, "or he doesn't perform. That's the rule."

Even though Clarence knew this guy could shut down the show, he blew up. Flinging his arms about, he started hollering, "That's ridicalus! Stevie's card ain't expired! That's ridicalus!"

It was a stalemate until Esther showed up a few minutes later. When the union rep repeated his demand to her, she simply said, "Oh. Okay, we'll take care of that right now."

She wrote the man a check and he left. She looked at me. "That's the way it should have been handled. It doesn't do any good to fight with them. We owe it, let's pay it."

Recognizing all that needed to be done for Stevie's well being, I gradually assumed more and more management responsibility. It also gave me opportunities to teach Stevie lessons related to the business side of his work. As well as teaching him school lessons, I wanted him to learn independence as both a performer and a person.

Math and a trip to England combined in a study of British currency. Stevie learned to exchange his two dollar and fifty cent weekly allowance into shillings—which everyone at Motown jokingly renamed "chittlins." If Stevie wanted a Coke or to buy his mother a gift, it would have been quicker for me to make the purchase, but it would have deprived him of the experience of figuring exchange prices and counting the payment and change. If we were taking the train or subway, I gave him the money and sent him to buy our tickets. When musicians were recruited or paid, when hotels had to be booked and travel reservations made, I wanted Stevie right there learning how it was all done. I can't think of anything I didn't relate directly to his education.

* * *

Within a year of taking on so many additional duties beyond teaching, the pressure took its mental and physical toll. Motown, unfortunately, hadn't offered to pay me any more. I liked the autonomy I had, but didn't like not being compensated for all the extra work.

In the spring of 1965, knowing it was well deserved, I asked Esther for a raise. She took my request to Berry, who told her he'd get back to me. I waited, but repeatedly told Esther I would quit if I didn't get the raise. Gordy continued to ignore me. Neither he nor Esther believed I'd walk out on Stevie. After two months, my patience wore out.

Berry and Esther were both shocked when I walked off the job that July. Berry was out of town on business and I didn't expect anything to be resolved until he returned the following week. Then tragedy struck. Louceye, Esther's younger and Berry's older sister, suddenly died of a cerebral hemorrhage.

I hadn't known Louceye well in the eighteen months I'd been with Motown, because our work rarely brought us together. But whenever she saw me at the office, no matter how busy she was, Louceye always took time to chat. She was genuinely interested in what was going on in my life as much as in Stevie's. Her death saddened us all.

I went to the funeral home to pay my respects. Berry shook my hand and quietly said, "I didn't expect to see you. I really appreciate your being here."

The way he spoke told me he was both surprised and pleased to see me, since I'd been away from my job for at least two weeks by then. But it never crossed my mind that in times of difficulty such an issue should separate people who cared about each other.

On my way out a short time later, Esther was also leaving. She offered me a ride home in one of Berry's chauffeured white Cadillacs. I said little, not wanting to intrude on her grief and thoughts. But after a few moments, she turned to me. "By the way," she said, "Berry's agreed to your raise." To this day, I don't know why he changed his mind about giving me the raise, or why he did it then.

Gordy had a reputation for paying low wages and everybody complained about it. Even the stars, who certainly earned more than the office staff, were underpaid. But for years I thought I was the lowest paid person at Motown. What I didn't know was that I was being paid more than most of the other employees.

Not long ago, Beans Bowles set me straight. "You were one of the best paid guys at Motown and I was a little ticked because you made much more money than me."

That amazed me. But I was glad Beans delivered his comment with a hearty chuckle, making it clear he didn't hold it against me.

"Everybody in Motown was underpaid," he added. "It's not that they planned it that way. The compensation was very, very poor, but the other things—there's no price for the things that I learned. What wasn't paid for in money was made up in other things. I had a head start on most of the people in Motown because of I'd been involved in show business. But I didn't really learn anything about the corporate structure of the world until I was in Motown. That's been invaluable."

Some people at Motown then now claim Gordy never really cared about the artists, that he cared only about the money. "Hindsight is so good," Beans said of that attitude. "Today, nine out of ten performers will say that *now*. They've forgotten the days that they were begging to be a part of Motown."

Beans recalled how Berry signed some people—"just as children"—to keep them from hounding him. Some of them became successful. "But nine out of ten people he signed, they didn't have talent. And then after he had signed so many, some of the good ones got lost in the shuffle because there were so many—three hundred people was the staff we had."

Motown had an abundance of talent to promote, and Gordy was ingenious when it came to getting their records on the air. Radio stations were allowed to play no more than three records on any one label in an hour. Without time to read each label, DJs learned to recognize them by color.

During the '60s, Motown grew to nine record labels, each in a different color. Stevie's songs were on Tamla, Martha and the Vandellas were released on Gordy Records, the Supremes on Motown, and so on. Using so many different labels, the company got far more than three songs on the air every hour. The more airplay Motown had, the more records were sold and the more money everybody made.

Motown's standard contract paid performers a royalty of one-and-one-half to two cents per record side for each sale. Really hot artists sometimes received three cents, which was big money. When a record was a million seller, artists thought they were going to be millionaires on that penny-and-a-half. It really wasn't bad pay for a single artist like Stevie, but if there were five people in the group, like the Temptations, that one-and-one-half cents had to be split five ways. And out of those earnings came expenses, which often caused more grumbling.

"Berry didn't steal a thing," Beans insisted. "Esther and I set up a system where the road manager handled records and we knew what money they spent on the road so we could keep our facts straight. I personally worked very hard on that system so that when they came back, I was able to detect fraud. Like if they spent eighty cents and put an extra dollar ahead of it, to make it look like it was an dollar and eighty cents."

All the performers assumed they could spend money any way they wanted. Then when they returned from a road trip and learned they'd cleared only a few hundred dollars profit, they didn't want to believe it. "They'd say Motown took the money," Beans remembers. "But if any money came up missing it was because they overspent or that road manager put something over on us."

I doubt it happened often because the bookkeeping records I had to keep for were so meticulously detailed. If anything, there were usually shortages that had to be repaid. And when that happened to me, it came out of my paycheck. I never wanted the reputation of having anyone being suspicious about my handling of money for Stevie or Motown.

Occasionally, my vision contributed to losses I had to reimburse. I'd been known to overpay musicians—counting out pay in a dimly lit backstage is difficult enough but with my visual impairment, I'd sometimes think a fifty dollar bill was a twenty, or a hundred was a ten. Funny, those fellows never once corrected me.

Probably my worst experience was in Birmingham, Alabama. Clarence called and woke me at two o'clock in the morning, wanting an advance. I couldn't understand why he hadn't asked before we'd left the show that night, but I dragged myself out of bed to meet him in the hotel lobby. I counted out the money from an envelope, we talked for a minute, and I went back upstairs to bed.

The next morning, I realized I'd left my cash envelope, with seven hundred dollars in it, on the lobby table. I was sick. Even though I knew it wouldn't help, I called the police. Adding insult to injury, the investigator who came out reviewed in minute detail every problem our show had caused for his department, including the nasty fight some fans got into outside the theater that resulted in several knifings. He made it very clear he wasn't sympathetic and certainly wasn't in the mood to do much investigating on my behalf.

Everyone younger than eighteen and under a Motown contract had to have a court appointed legal guardian. I don't know about the others, but in Stevie's case the guardian was Berry Gordy Enterprises. As BGE administrator, that made the company his guardian as well as his manager. Maybe one of the reasons some Motown performers think they didn't get as much money as they should have is that arrangement could be seen as the fox guarding the hen house.

Because of his handicap, the court also appointed an administrator for Stevie, but I don't know why or even who it was. In all my years with Stevie, I never met the person who was supposedly watching out for his financial interests.

At that time, Stevie was generating a tremendous amount of money, which remained under the guardian's control until he turned twenty-one. Stevie was never privy to or interested in the accounting of the revenue he generated. But then, I don't recall that financial statements were ever distributed to anyone by Motown. Other performers might have requested them, but I know none went to Stevie. If they had, they'd have gone to Lula, who would have turned to me to explain them.

I think one reason Motown performers became disgruntled about money was because they didn't understand where it came from or went. Managers knew how expensive it was to be on the road, but the performers had no idea. If the company had informed and educated Motown's acts on the cost of doing business, some of them probably wouldn't have moved to other labels and managers. They'd have known what was going on. But all they saw was that Motown was spending "their" money, with no idea of how it was being used. That's when paranoia would set in.

Before I became heavily involved in Stevie's management, I fell victim to that delusion myself. During the Motown Revue in England, Clarence Paul convinced both me and Stevie that Motown was ripping Stevie off. I called Berry and told him I wanted to talk with him about Stevie's contract. Typically, he said we'd get together later. Days passed and I was certain he'd either forgotten or was ignoring me, which only fueled my belief that Clarence was right.

Then one afternoon, as I passed outside Berry's hotel room, he called to me over the balcony rail. "Ted, you still want that meeting? Get Clarence and Stevie and meet me in the restaurant."

The four of sat down and Berry asked, "Now, what's the problem?"

The days I'd spent thinking about what Clarence claimed had given my irritation time to build. "I understand Stevie isn't making any money on this trip. He ought to be making more money than he used to, and now I understand you're actually paying him less than before."

"No." Berry said calmly, "Those aren't the facts. I have the facts and you don't."

Then he patiently explained the details of Stevie's contract, how much he was earning, what expenses were and how much income Stevie would clear on the tour. All three of us were rather dumbfounded that Clarence's information, based solely on office rumor, was totally inaccurate.

I was embarrassed, but impressed that Berry discussed things so openly and without rancor. As the meeting broke up, Berry gave me a piece of advice. "Always remember to make sure that you have the right information."

From that day on, I made it a point to verify my facts before I acted.

Berry worked just as hard behind the scenes as any Motown performer did in front of a microphone. He became famous in his own right, but Berry never acted the star when he was with us. He was a part of the team, and that was healthy. Still, gossip fueled a constant friction within the company. The fame-building days the performers often recall fondly make it sound as if Motown was one big happy family. It was, but even the happiest families sometimes have fights. There was a lot of suspicion, a lot of back-stabbing, as the company mushroomed. What many choose to forget, or just not talk about, is that Motown was made up of young people with very little formal education. They performed before adoring audiences and heard their songs on the radio. Based solely on those ego-building factors and without any knowledge of how business finances work, rumors would spread like an infectious disease.

Mary Wells was one of the first singers Gordy made famous. Motown trained her to perform flawlessly on stage, explaining why every move was important. But no one ever explained the rest of the effort required to make her a star. She became certain that Motown was getting rich at her expense. Thinking she could find a better company to handle her, she left, and it marked the end of her singing career. Later Martha Reeves quit, upset for the same reasons, and her career never again attained the heights Gordy had achieved for the Vandellas.

The problems that become issues with Mary Wells, Martha Reeves some of the others really didn't happen with Stevie because I made it a point to understand what was going on. Everyone in Motown worked hard and no one received the pay they really deserved. I honestly don't believe Gordy or anyone else ever set out to abuse the staff. And I know no one realized the added difficulties involved working with a blind person. If Stevie had been sighted, I would have had plenty of time to accomplish a multitude of things.

* * *

I was trying to teach Stevie to grow into independence, so he would not need me or anybody else to handle his life. I tried to keep myself on the sidelines, concerned about every move he made and everything he did. Like Bartholomew Cubbins, I wore a vast number of hats: teacher, coach, surrogate parent, family advisor, Motown employee, road manager, valet, and more—yet I tried never to let Stevie or anyone else know how draining all those roles were. The time it took to do my job was made doubly difficult simply because Stevie's blindness required alternative methods others didn't require, and kept me by his side almost all the time.

And it was several years before I started getting help. Whenever Stevie performed, my first worry was finding good musicians to work the show. It was a relief to finally be told I could hire a permanent guitar player to tour with us. I never found one who'd last more than a few shows. Getting musicians who were talented, reliable and morally fit to be on the road with a teenager like Stevie was always difficult.

The one exception was a fellow I never expected it of. "Beau" Bohannon was a drummer I found in 1966. Beau, in the beginning, was an absolute pain in the behind, and the last person I ever expected to be a stable influence on Stevie.

When we first met, I liked him for two reasons. He was only a few years older than Stevie, with a clean, decent personality. And he told me that he owned his own drums. So I hired him for Stevie's appearance at a fund-raiser in Washington, D.C., hosted by the famous and acerbic reporter Walter Winchell. When we arrived for the gig, something was missing.

"Where're your drums?" I asked.

"Oh, um," Beau hemmed and hawed, then admitted, "Uh, I don't own any."

"What do you mean you don't own any drums?" The show was being set up. I was so angry I nearly screamed. I fired him on the spot and he actually broke down and cried. "You're done," I insisted. "You're out of here. You lied to me. We're supposed to pay you, and now we're supposed to rent you drums, too? Forget it!"

I stuck to my guns. But I couldn't get rid of him. For weeks he'd call me, begging for another chance.

It was now was close to Christmas, when Motown presented a series of holiday shows at Detroit's Fox Theater. Once a magnificent old place, the Fox was on its last legs, showing second- and third-run movies. Motown's two-day Christmas Revues were the only live shows being performed there at the time. Playing for our hometown crowd was great, but I hated those two days backstage with a passion. Every relative and every friend of every act, every musician, every producer and every performer showed up, and wanted free tickets. It was impossible to get Stevie's schoolwork done at the theater because it was continuous, wall-to-wall party time.

During the first afternoon show, I stood backstage watching Stevie perform. I turned around and damn, there was Beau, standing right next to me. He'd come all the way from Washington D.C. Talk about persistence!

"Give me another chance," he begged. "Come on, please?"

"No, Beau, I've made up my mind. You're done."

But he wasn't. Somehow, he got to Esther. That evening she came over and asked, "Ted, why don't you give Beau another chance? I've talked to him. I feel sorry for him."

That didn't surprise me. I knew how empathetic Esther could be, especially to Bo's sorrowful, hangdog expression. I sighed in resignation when Esther said we'd rent drums until he'd earned enough to buy his own.

Looking back on it, that turned out to be one of the best decisions I was ever forced to go along with. Beau turned out to be a splendid guy and a great companion for Stevie, which helped my peace of mind. To this day, I credit him with averting a situation that could easily have tarnished Stevie's image.

Girls were always after Stevie. As much as he loved it, that presented its own set of problems. Even though he was still a skinny and somewhat gawky teen, the girls went wild over him. On one trip in Canada I opened the hotel room door when I heard a knock, and half a dozen teenage girls burst in. Stevie was seated on the edge of bed, and they climbed all over it and him, rubbing him in some highly inappropriate places. He loved it, and giggled and chatted playfully the whole time. Every time I peeled one of the girls off, the others were on him again.

Shortly after Beau became Stevie's drummer we did a show in Chicago. A sixteen-year-old girl came backstage to meet Stevie, who was also sixteen. She was well spoken, had very good manners and was nicely dressed. I was impressed with the young lady and could tell Stevie didn't need to see her to tell she was a knockout.

She invited Stevie to her home for dinner the next day. Well, for Stevie it seemed to be love at first sight and he asked if he could go. Insisting that I'd go along as chaperone, I agreed because I liked him having the opportunity to be around kids outside of the music industry.

Our dinner with her parents went well and Stevie invited the girl to visit him at our hotel the next afternoon. That was fine with me, because I'd make sure Beau would be with them.

The next morning, Beau came to me. His voice was worried. "That girl phoned Stevie. I overheard the conversation. She's bringing her uncle. He's a photographer."

Right away, red flags went up in my mind. I knew it might just be an innocent situation, but a gorgeous teenage girl in a hotel room with Stevie Wonder and a professional photographer sounded like a bombshell waiting to explode—either in the newspapers or possibly in demands on Motown.

It was a serious possibility. I'll never forget when a girl told Stevie's mother she was pregnant with Stevie's baby. I didn't buy it, and neither did Lula.

"If he comes out black, blind and playing the harmonica, then I'll believe you!" Lula yelled at her. No one ever heard from the girl again.

Now, my responsibility was clear but difficult. I had to be the bad guy and put a stop the date. I conjured up a reason why Stevie had to call her and cancel. He didn't question me because unexpected things often cropped up for us to take care of.

I may have been absolutely wrong that day. I just knew I had to avoid anything that could put Stevie in a compromising position. Whether I ended a relationship that could have been important to Stevie, I'll never know. I've always been sorry it happened. But I was glad Beau was watching out for his friend.

Workout, Stevie, Workout

"Handicapped people get a lot of applause just for being handicapped. Stevie lost a lot of applause because people started doubting he was blind.."
                                                    — *Esther Gordy Edwards*

*T*he *Ed Sullivan Show* was the No. 1 television program in the nation during the '60s. In its heyday, more than 30-million viewers tuned in every Sunday night from eight to nine to watch acts that ran the gamut from opera to pop music, from magic to vaudeville, jugglers and comics, scenes from Broadway shows and ballet—all performed live. Only the best performers were invited. Mary Wells had been the first Motown artist to appear on national TV, but for "Little Stevie Wonder" to be Motown's first act scheduled by Ed Sullivan in 1964 was, as Ed was mimicked to say, "a really big *sh-ew*."

Ardena, Stevie and I met at the Detroit airport on a Friday to fly to New York and prepare for Sunday night's show. A friend drove me to the airport and we chatted while I waited to board the plane. All of a sudden I realized Ardena and Stevie were gone. And so was the plane. I was in a panic.

Hurrying frantically from gate to gate, I managed to find another flight half an hour later. Landing at LaGuardia, I repeatedly paged Ardena, but neither she nor Stevie were anywhere to be found. I made my way to the gate where their flight should have arrived, hoping to learn what had happened to them. I did—their plane was still in the air. My frenzied trip had actually gotten me to New York an hour ahead of them.

139

Ardena was shocked to see me waiting, and Stevie's relief was palpable. Throughout the flight Stevie was clearly concerned, she said, repeatedly asking, "Where's Mr. Hull? He's got my clothes! He's got the band's music! He's got the expense money! What are we going to do?" And she didn't know.

Back on schedule again, we headed to the theater, where Ardena and I were to meet with the producers and discuss Stevie's performance. Excited and primed for a friendly planning session, we walked right into more trouble.

Before leaving Detroit, we were told Stevie's number would be *Fingertips*—the one song every teenager in America associated with him. Wrong, said the extremely conservative producers, who could not have cared less what Stevie's fans, or Motown for that matter, wanted. Stevie, they flatly stated, would sing a number more pleasing to older viewers, such as *On The Sunny Side of the Street*, from his most recent— and deservedly ignored—album, *With A Song In My Heart*.

Ardena and I argued our position politely at first, then more stridently as the producers made it clear they wouldn't agree. Finally, there was nothing to do but call Berry. Ardena and I, worried and tense, walked out of the meeting. While Ardena placed the call, I told Stevie about the situation. Even though he was a fairly seasoned performer, appearing on *The Ed Sullivan Show* had him a bit tense, and this news only upset him more.

Ardena's conversation with the office was short. "You stick to your guns," she was told. "You tell them we know what the people want to hear. And you work this out. It's important."

It was never suggested we threaten to pull Stevie from the show, and we didn't want to push the producers into doing that for us. We felt our backs were to the wall, but back into the conference room we went. The longer we got nowhere, the thicker the tension grew before we were able to reach a compromise.

Unfortunately, the solution was far from ideal for Stevie. The producers would agree to *Fingertips* only if it was shortened considerably by their own arrangers. By rehearsal time, Stevie had only a few hours to learn a totally new version of the song he'd been singing for three years. And the arrangement was so badly chopped up that it should have been re-titled *Fingerstubs*.

Still, the disagreement barely tarnished our excitement over Stevie's appearance on television's most important show. A real thrill for me was that mellow-voiced Patti Page, one of my very favorite singers, was also on the bill. Meeting during rehearsal, she was as pleasant and friendly as I'd dreamed. But my fantasies about this gorgeous blonde in her 30's were tarnished when I got near enough to see her face. I'd never seen so much makeup on anyone in my life. I tried to tell myself it was probably for the cameras, but even with my poor eyesight I finally understood just what "painted lady" meant. I guess it was even more of a shock because Motown's girl singers used hardly any makeup at all, even when they were on stage.

Smooth singers like Patti Page were a staple on *The Ed Sullivan Show*. Ed and his producers thought like a lot of people then—that rock 'n' roll was *not* here to stay. By the mid-'60s, Ed and his producers realized the teen audience was too large to dismiss. When rock singers or groups appeared, it meant only that their ratings were too big to ignore. As far as Ed was concerned, both the acts and their teen fans would be tolerated only as long as they were tightly controlled.

Like Stevie, every rock group or singer had to shorten lyrics or clean up their acts. When Elvis appeared on his show in 1957, Ed insisted the cameras show him only above the waist, so viewers wouldn't be subjected to Presley's "vulgar" hip-grinding. When the Beatles appeared, just a year before Stevie, Ed sounded like a stern father, admonishing girls in the audience about their frenzied screaming. The Rolling Stones' were forced to revise lyrics in their six appearances, but having to change the words to *Satisfaction*, their huge hit, because the producers deemed them too "sexual," was the last time they gave into such a demand ... and the last time they stood on Ed's stage.

The Doors made only one appearance. They, too, had to agree to water down the words to *Light My Fire*, which Sullivan deemed too suggestive of drugs. But Jim Morrison sang "Girl, we couldn't get much higher," anyway. Ed was more than angry and had the group informed they'd just lost their chance to ever appear on his show. Morrison's response was, "Hey man, we just *did* the Sullivan show."

Not all rock stars were so nonchalant about losing such exposure. The fact that stars from Stevie to the Stones accepted such restrictions was proof of Ed Sullivan's importance.

Even though we'd done battle with his producers, Ardena and I remained in awe of Ed Sullivan himself. Just before Stevie was scheduled to go on, Ardena worked up her courage and asked, "Mr. Sullivan? Could you please mention that Stevie is from Motown Record Company?"

Her hands were clasped to her chest like a timid little girl. Like a teasing uncle, Ed grinned and pinched her cheek. "Oh, you want a *commercial*, don't you, honey?"

Ardena didn't get her "commercial"—Ed's introduction was short and simple: "Next, here's Little Stevie Wonder, outta Detroit."

All of us always taught Stevie that performing was like any other work: you just go out and do your job. But with the pressure of the negotiations, having to quickly learn a completely new version of *Fingertips*, and the show's very real significance to both him and Motown, Stevie knew this was the most momentous program he'd done to date. He became increasingly tense throughout the arguments and rehearsals.

It was the first time I'd seen him so obviously affected by backstage difficulties, and from that day on I made a point to shield him from such problems. I was extremely concerned that his anxiety would be apparent on stage. But once he was on stage, I was proud to see that, even at the young age of fourteen, Stevie's professionalism was so keen that not one viewer ever realized his nervousness.

Even with *Fingertips* so brutally shortened, Stevie's appearance was an incredible high. Seconds after getting back to the dressing room, Barney Ales rushed in. We'd had no idea that Motown's super sales manager would be in the audience. Grabbing Stevie in a bear hug and lifting him right off the ground, he hollered, "You did it! You did it!"

Stevie threw back his head in laughter. "What did you expect?"

* * *

Stevie's musical performances were invariably outstanding on television. Other aspects of his appearances weren't always so successful. One area where he sometimes drew criticism from Gordy was his inability to do a good in-depth interview on a talk show.

While *Fingertips* was still at the top, Stevie was a guest on the *Tonight* show, then hosted by comedian Joey Bishop. Typically, Stevie knocked out the audience with a song. Afterward, he sat down on the show's famous couch to chat with Joey. Following a few moments of light banter, Joey turned serious.

"Stevie," he asked, "just what is 'soul'?"

"Well," Stevie answered, "the only soul I'm aware of is the sole of my shoe."

Listening from the Green Room, all I could do was grimace. "Soul" was a word just entering the American lexicon and I understood that Joey wanted to know what made a song or a thing "soulful." Stevie's flip response was an attempt at humor, and from both Joey's and the audience's reactions, I knew it hadn't worked. For the rest of the interview, Joey seemed to be at a disadvantage in trying to make the conversation interesting. After only another minute or two, Joey asked Stevie to sing another song. It was his polite way of ending the strained interview and nudging the boy off stage.

That was one of the times Gordy wasn't pleased. I felt responsible, that I should have prepared Stevie better. But I also realized that, because of his immense talent, people often forgot he was so young. He'd done very few live interviews and simply didn't have an adult's knowledge, vocabulary or experience to draw upon in such situations.

Another TV appearance which didn't go well was the fault of the host, not Stevie. *The Mike Douglas Show* was a popular afternoon variety/talk show broadcast from Cleveland. Douglas, a popular "boy" singer with Big Bands in the late '40s and '50s, had one of the two highest rated daytime shows in the '60s. The other was hosted by Merv Griffin, who'd also started out on the Big Band circuit.

When he was invited to Douglas's show, Stevie was just emerging from the hitless two- year drought after *Fingertips*. We were excited about reaching a broad national audience again. The plan was for Stevie to do a tune, leave the stage, return later with a second song and then a chat with Mike and the show's other guests.

Mike opened the show and introduced Stevie, who, as usual, left the middle-class female audience in cheers. After Stevie returned backstage, we watched as Mike interviewed an elderly lady who'd done something unusual enough to attract the show's interest. She was a darling charmer, and Douglas basked in all the adoration she poured on him. At a commercial break just before Stevie's second number, Douglas stuck his head into the room where we waited.

"Hey, fellas, I don't want to make you angry or anything, but this lady's doing so good we're not going to have Stevie come back out. Sorry." He started to leave.

Stevie was disappointed, but I was just plain mad—Mike's self-effacing manner with guests on the set was a complete turn-about from the pompous and self-important way I'd seen him use with his crew and guests off stage. Instead of prudently letting the situation slide, the Papa Bear in me bared his teeth. I knew how hard Stevie had worked to get ready for this show and I was angry that he was getting the brush-off. I didn't care how famous Mike Douglas was. I blew my top and let the guy know just what I thought. It didn't do any good and I know it was a poor way for me to handle things. Stevie never was invited back, but I didn't care. I was sick and tired of seeing people treat Stevie like an expendable product, with no regard for his feelings.

Dick Clark's *American Bandstand* rock/dance party was, of course, a national sensation in the mid-'60s, with good reason. Every time Stevie appeared on his show we all had a great time. Clark's personality was the exact opposite of people like Douglas, who operated from the standpoint of "What's in it for me?."

Dick had a way of putting everyone at ease, making every guest feel like a cherished friend. Yet at the same time, he had a low-key way of maintaining total control over the show. As a result, performers were glad to do whatever was asked. He'd respectfully listen to suggestions, and we respected his decisions because he was incredibly good at what he did. And he did a lot for Motown.

I know Dick realized the importance Motown played in his early success, too. I think his fame has continued all these years for the same reason that Berry Gordy was able to make Motown such an institution—both men understood that they and the artists together created something much larger than could be attained independently.

From a teenager's point of view, Dick Clark was one of the most important men in the country when it came to the music they wanted to hear. *American Bandstand* was the weekly, live national dance party everyone wanted to attend, whether or not they lived in its hometown of Philadelphia. Radio, on the other hand, was every teen's constant companion, delivering rock around the clock.

Every city we visited that had a local station meant a chance for Stevie to appear on the radio, too. And he loved it. Stevie actually gave some serious consideration to becoming a disc jockey for a while. He had a great time with the DJs, learning to work the boards and spinning records.

Any time we met a new DJ, Stevie got a kick out of creating some confusion in the sound booth. Before the interview, I'd peer through the booth window and describe as much as I could to Stevie. An absolute master at timing his pranks, Stevie would work the interview till just the right moment to lean into the mike and comment, "Gee, that's a sharp red tie you've got on," or "Man, I really like that plaid shirt you're wearing today."

Every single DJ was totally flummoxed and reduced to stammers. Some were so naive that their jaws literally dropped. Here was a kid they'd been told was totally blind, complimenting their appearance! Not one of them ever knew how to react with the mike open. As soon as they could get a record on, quite a few of them blurted, "How'd you do that? Are you really blind?" Only then would we let them in on the joke.

Stevie wasn't the only one I'd coach before interviews. Whenever possible, I'd prompt the DJ or reporter about topics to bring up. Stevie mesmerized people because of his youth and talent, but I wanted them to see beyond his music and blindness. So often my friends would tell me later, "I heard Stevie on that show yesterday. Boy, he talks just like you do! He says the same things you say." I've got to admit, such comments pleased me. Radio interviews in particular were great places for him to talk about his schooling and help dispel misconceptions about blindness. Some people—our driver Gene Shelby included, remained convinced that Stevie could tell colors by touching them.

In other ways, Stevie's self-sufficiency did create confusion with the public. One of the first things I went to work on when I became Stevie's teacher was making it possible for him to navigate the stage without a sighted guide. At times it was necessary for me or someone else to walk him onto the set, but whenever possible the instruments and cables were laid out in a specific pattern that Stevie knew. We worked out sound cues for the musicians to play, so Stevie knew where to move next. Neither Stevie nor I ever wanted him to capitalize on the pity-factor so many handicapped people have to contend with, and it worked. Too well, sometimes. Like the DJ's caught off-guard, fans often wondered if his blindness was being faked.

* * *

Every region had its most popular DJs but only a few ever attained national fame. Probably the most famous was California's Wolfman Jack. Right up there, too, was New York's Cousin Brucie. And a third was Murray the K.

Murray was one of a handful of DJs who could make or break a record on the charts during the '60s. He knew it, and soon believed that he was as important, if not more so, than the singers and groups he put on the air. Soon, radio wasn't enough to satisfy Murray's ego, who next established himself as a successful promoter. Probably his greatest achievement was bringing the Beatles to the United States in February 1964.

Later that year, Murray scheduled a week-long show at the Brooklyn Fox theater. Dozens of top acts were lined up—including Stevie, Martha Reeves and the Vandellas, Marvin Gaye, the Temptations and the Supremes from Motown, plus Little Anthony & the Imperials, the Lovin' Spoonful, Phil Spector's Ronettes, and other hit groups. Clarence Paul and I accompanied Stevie.

We quickly discovered that Murray's intention was to spotlight himself, not the acts. Everything that was sung and everything that was done was designed to proclaim Murray the K *"the"* star. One scene was staged as if he were the lead actor in a little play, on a set resembling a small sitting room. Every one of these famous singers and musicians was to sit or lay on the floor, surrounding Murray's throne-like chair like adoring children.

Martha Reeves loved it—in her book, she wrote, "You'd find yourselves acting like children together, falling down, rolling around, carrying signs, playing 'musical stools,' dancing and laughing ... it was thrilling and electric from beginning to end."

Maybe Martha was at a different show, because no one I was around considered it fun. In fact, Marvin Gaye was so offended that he stormed out of rehearsal. And I didn't blame him. I don't remember exactly what Stevie was supposed to do, but it was something Clarence Paul and I considered absolutely asinine and Stevie found embarrassing. Clarence pitched a major fit about it to Murray's crew. Stevie was a star, Clarence insisted, and deserved to be treated with respect. The stage director refused to make any changes not authorized by his boss, so the three of us set off to demand that Murray put a stop to the shabby treatment Stevie was receiving.

As Motown's representatives, we knew Gordy would fully support us in our argument. Unfortunately, our physical presence did little to support an aura of authority as we navigated the backstage hallways. Clarence, who'd recently broken his ankle, sported a cast up to his knee and was confined to a wheelchair. The dimly lit hallways, strewn with cables and props, were so dark I couldn't see well enough to lead the way. And of course, Stevie couldn't see at all.

Acting as navigator, Clarence rode in front, with Stevie pushing the wheelchair as Clarence told him which way to go and what to watch out for. I brought up the rear, my hand resting on Stevie's shoulder, and scrambling to avoid obstacles Clarence alerted us to. We formed a sorry-looking procession. I'm sure it did much to enhance our stature when we finally were allowed into Murray's palatial dressing room—the lame, the blind and the partially sighted, descending upon him in a high state of indignation.

I knew Clarence was hot-headed enough to really create big trouble for us, so I insisted on handling the discussion. In my best business-like manner, I explained that what was being rehearsed was totally different from what we'd been told to expect, and that Stevie was to be treated with the consideration his star status deserved.

Murray stood pat. "This is my show," he growled. "This is the way it's going to be."

At that point, Clarence completely lost his temper and threatened to pull Stevie from the bill.

"Look, damn it," Murray snarled. "I've got your name on the contract. And the contract says that this is the way it's going to be."

Clarence wasn't about to back off from the argument. I interrupted, "Let's leave it for right now, until I can find out what's on the contract."

I called Esther, who was in charge of all of Stevie's contracts. As I described what was taking place, she became as displeased about the situation as we were.

"How obligated are we?" I asked. She put me on hold while she found the contract. As she read it aloud over the phone, it became obvious we were bound by an iron-clad agreement. If Stevie—or any other Motown performer, for that matter—dropped out of the show for any reason short of death, Murray the K could file suit against the company. There was simply nothing any of us could do. What Murray the Ego wanted, Murray the K would get.

I was forced to admit to Stevie and Clarence that the man held all the cards. There was nothing we could do except survive the week's humiliation.

* * *

Out of all the years I traveled with Stevie, there were only two shows we missed. Considering the trouble I often had arranging transportation, it amazes me it didn't happen more often.

During a strike against the major airlines in the '60s, we needed to leave a show in Chicago, which ended at one a.m., and be at the Apollo Theater in New York City the next day for an eight a.m. rehearsal. After hours on the phone tracking down every possible lead, I located a private pilot with a Cessna who agreed to fly us. As soon as we could make it to the airport after Stevie's last performance, he, Beau Bohannon and I piled all the equipment—meaning uniforms, Bo's drums, Stevie's school books, everything—and ourselves into that tiny four-seater. Packed to the rafters, we managed to get it all in, everything but Stevie's tape recorder. The only place for Beau to sit was on his drum case, but neither Stevie nor I was much more comfortable

When we landed at LaGuardia a few hours later, a skycap arrived to help us unload. From the way his eyes got bigger and bigger as more and more stuff came out of the plane, he must have thought we were one of those circus acts where dozens of clowns come piling out of a tiny car. When Stevie finally managed to extricate himself from behind all the equipment, the skycap's jaw really dropped. He may have been used to helping stars with their bags, but he'd obviously never seen one crammed in a plane like a sardine in a tin can.

Still, we made it to the theater on time. The time we didn't was in the middle of a run at Atlantic City's famous Steel Pier. What still ticks me off is that no one believed me when I told them it was going to happen.

The Steel Pier was a prestigious place to play, with a ballroom and separate stage for simultaneous performances. The Pier contracted with one of the most fabulous house bands we ever had the good fortune to work with. And the stars appearing during the same dates as Stevie were among the most impressive he'd ever been invited to join—Count Basie and Frank Sinatra, Jr. Since all three shows were separately scheduled, I was able to get Stevie over to see Basie perform twice, and it was an incredible experience for us both.

But the trip presented problems right from the start. With no direct flights into Atlantic City, Stevie, Beau and I flew a complicated schedule. We reached New York in the evening, planning to catch a puddle-jumper connection to our destination. Double-checking everything as it came off the baggage carousel at LaGuardia, we discovered a serious problem. The music hadn't been packed. I'd assigned each of us responsibility for certain items. It had been up to Stevie to bringing the band's arrangements. He'd left them at home.

Angrily, I ordered Beau and a contrite Stevie to catch the flight to Atlantic City, then phoned Detroit. Rebecca Giles, who to this day is still Berry's fantastic secretary, knew the situation was grave. Stevie's first show was scheduled for one o'clock the next afternoon. She promised to have the music picked up immediately from Stevie's house and sent on the next possible flight. All I could do was sit, wait, and pray it would arrive in time.

Knowing it couldn't arrive before early morning, I tried without success to get some sleep in the uncomfortable airport chairs. As the hours passed, I really began to worry. Until I had the sheet music in hand, I couldn't even make arrangements to get myself to Atlantic City. As the wee hours of morning turned to dawn, and dawn turned to late morning, the tension became almost unbearable.

The package finally arrived. But there was little more than an hour to make it to the Steel Pier. Hurriedly, I booked a private charter. Even though the flight was short, time seemed to move much faster than the plane. When we touched down, I was out and running for a cab before the pilot shut down the engine.

By the time I reached backstage, there were only three minutes to show time. The place was packed—Stevie's show was completely sold out. Behind the stage curtain, the musicians were in their places, completely relaxed and ready to play. I handed the music to the house band director, who quickly passed it out as he told his musicians the order of the line-up.

Within seconds, and right on time, the curtain went up, the band started and I nearly collapsed in relief. It was amazing. The musicians were such pros, they played as if they'd been performing Stevie's tunes for years.

It was a world of difference, having professional musicians, instead of some of the terrible situations we got into with promoters who hired low-rate bands that couldn't read music. Stevie felt guilty for having created the trouble, and I let him know that he deserved to. I wasn't happy with him, just as any father would whose son had shirked an important responsibility. But I still felt responsible, knowing I should never have put a fifteen-year-old kid in charge of the most valuable thing we had to bring besides his school books.

Esther, though, saw it differently. When she came out later in the week to visit, she put her arm around Stevie's shoulder. Her voice was consoling. "You forgot the music, but that's okay. The problem is you just don't have enough people helping you."

She was right—and I'd been telling her just that for a long time. Unfortunately, nothing would change for years. And when it did, it wasn't for the better.

After that heart-stopping start, things rolled smoothly for a while. Frank Bryant, Junior Walker's one-and-only lead guitarist and a superb musician, was Stevie's main backup, which meant one less worry for me. The schedule was loose enough that I even had the chance to take Stevie, Frank and his wife out deep-sea fishing. Although Stevie had waded in the Atlantic and experienced the sound, smell and feel of the surf when we'd played in Fort Lauderdale, he'd never been out on the ocean. He'd never been fishing either, and hadn't even touched a fish.

I think I was the only one who enjoyed the half-day excursion, though. Frank and his wife both got seasick. Stevie was so exhausted from all the travel and shows he'd been doing that he fell asleep. Still, he was the only one who caught a fish that day, and I had to wake him when he hooked it. But then, the fish was only about six inches long, so it didn't put up a noticeable fight, either.

We were doing the usual number of three or four shows a day, starting early in the afternoon and finishing around midnight. Things continued smoothly till the office called. A big-name New York disc jockey was doing a television special, I was told. Would I please take Stevie to the city for a morning taping at Yankee Stadium?

"No," I said. I knew we'd be hard pressed to make it back to the Steel Pier in time for the day's one p.m. show.

This was not a request, I was told politely, it was a command. My objections would be noted, but I was to take Stevie and Beau and do the television taping. No ifs, ands, or buts.

So I followed orders. We finished that night's performance well after midnight, took a cab to the bus station and climbed aboard the Greyhound. By then it was about three a.m. When we reached the stadium in the morning, all three of us we were thoroughly wiped out.

Filming began right away but I realized quickly that our schedule meant nothing. The producer insisted on shooting Stevie's performance over and over, and over. As the morning dragged on, I became more and more concerned about making it back for the show.

Mentally figuring the time we'd need to get from the stadium to the airport by cab, fly back to Atlantic City, catch a taxi and make it to the Steel Pier, I knew we'd need more than two hours for the trip. Traveling by bus, it had taken nearly six hours to make the one-way trip. I knew I knew that if we'd had a car, the 130 mile distance would have been an easy drive. Such a simple solution wasn't available to us, though. Beau was under 21, which meant the agencies wouldn't allow him to rent a vehicle. Because of my visual handicap, I was denied the right to rent a car, which Beau could have driven. Thank God the Americans with Disabilities Act has outlawed such a silly restriction that hampered blind people for so many years.

My only choice was to charter a twin-engine Piper Cherokee, and hope we'd get back in time. At nearly eleven-thirty, I finally put my foot down and told the producer the taping was over. We were leaving. I knew we were cutting things close, but it began to look like we'd make it.

Then the pilot overshot his first landing attempt. The tower stuck us back in the traffic pattern. That sealed the deal—we didn't hit the tarmac for another half-hour. By the time we reached the Steel Pier, we were nearly an hour late for the show. The fans were long gone and the promoter had been forced to refund every ticket.

The promoter was not a man we could afford to anger. Along with being powerful enough to control who played the prestigious Steel Pier, he also booked major acts for state fairs around the country. When I arrived at his office to see what kind of trouble we were in, he was outraged. I really didn't blame him. First he threatened to sue Motown for breach of contract. Then he insisted we would make up his financial loss by playing several state fairs for an absolutely ridiculous price.

His terms were so unfavorable that I knew the office would never agree. Still, I called International Talent Management, Motown's booking division. Just as I expected, they flat-out refused to accept the man's demands. The promoter and I finished the week's run without speaking to each other. Stevie never again appeared at the Steel Pier or at any other venue controlled by that promoter.

Yes, it was just so much fun being the one in the middle at times like that. But my conscience was clear. I'd laid it out right up front that the trip into New York City was a bad idea.

When we were back in Detroit, Esther called me to her office. Before going in, I chatted a minute with her secretary. Emily mentioned that "some people" weren't happy about what had happened.

"I know," I admitted. "I did the best I could, but I'd already warned everybody it was going to be a problem."

Esther walked out of her office. "No, Ted," she said, "the problem is that you told them the truth."

The only other show we missed was a live TV rock 'n' roll dance program in Philadelphia. Our saving grace was that it was a local show and not *American Bandstand.*

Whenever I had the chance to bypass the major airlines, I liked using a local twin-engine service out of Detroit City Airport. Loving to fly as much as I did, those little planes were more fun and gave me better control over our schedule than the airlines. The trouble was, they often couldn't land in bad weather and on this flight we encountered it in spades. Surrounding the Philadelphia area was a severe storm that forced us to circle the airport endlessly until the weather cleared enough to land.

By the time we arrived at the television studio, the show was moments from ending. The stage manager was exceptionally understanding when I explained what happened. The emcee got Stevie on camera for no more than a minute, just enough time to ask a couple of questions and say, "Stevie, I understand that your plane couldn't land, so we really hope you'll come back some day."

People as gracious as that were what made all the struggles worthwhile. As I look back on those times, I wonder how we managed to do as much as we did with so little help. If I knew what I know today, I'd say one person just couldn't have done it. I guess I just did what I did because I didn't know it couldn't be done.

Music Talk

"Music can measure how broad our horizons are. My mind wants to see infinity."

— *Stevie Wonder*

Today, Stevie's reputation as a composer is as great as his fame as a musician. He hasn't reached the limits of his creativity and I doubt he ever will. Yet, when he first started at Motown, the most he might contribute to song writing was a melody phrase here or a verse punch line there.

From the beginning, Clarence Paul and Hank Cosby were the only two who really welcomed Stevie's musical suggestions. Clarence's main role at Motown was as a songwriter and producer. One of his first hits was Marvin Gaye's *Hitch Hike*, co-written with Marvin and Mickey Stevenson. Clarence was the motivating force who awakened Stevie's interest in song writing.

"You had to get Stevie in a mood to work," he recalled. "You had to kind of push him, and the more you pushed him the harder he worked."

There's no doubt in my mind that Clarence was the major influence on Stevie's artistic development. And the creativity the three of us shared was what I enjoyed the most. On the road, the first thing we'd ask every hotel desk clerk was, "Is there a piano?" A lot of times the answer would be, "Yes, but it's in the bar and you can't play it." As if a little thing like that would stop us. The next morning or early afternoon, before the bar opened and the piano was in use, we were right there at work.

Backstage in a dressing room or wherever we happened to be, we wrote and improvised, using whatever musical tools we had. Clarence used his voice to mimic piano runs, guitar riffs or bass. For percussion,

155

Stevie clapped or beat drumsticks on a table. He'd play melody on his harmonica.

(Stevie went through harmonicas like crazy. In the beginning, it was his main instrument and we were always running short of them. He'd come off the show and say, "Mr. Hull, the C note doesn't work anymore."

At first, Hoehner provided them for free to get publicity, but he went through them so fast that it quickly became a losing proposition for them.)

We toted around a very primitive keyboard—almost a toy, really, that ran on flashlight batteries and sounded like a cross between a concertina and a harmonica. If we'd had the fantastic portable keyboards available today, I think oh! what music we could have made. But when it comes down to it, even high-tech tools wouldn't have changed the songs Clarence, Stevie and I wrote.

The music Motown produced in the early and mid-1960s was on the cutting edge of rock. Compared to today's rock 'n' roll, those lyrics are so innocent that my wife Margaret now uses the Motown library in a music therapy program for multi-handicapped preschoolers.

People just didn't need blatantly sexual lyrics. The songwriters wanted to deliver romance and poetry. I remember Eddie and Brian Holland and Lamont Dozier—that famous team known as Holland Dozier and Holland—telling a reporter who asked about inspiration for their songs, "We like to write songs that turn women on."

What's almost laughable is that some of the Motown lyrics, compared to what else was being written then, *were* considered racy. Double entendre lyrics could be caught by sophisticated adult listeners, yet still came across squeaky clean to young teens like Stevie. Still, most of Motown's songs were simple, sweet and innocent. What Motown looked for was something unique—a new idea, sound, chord progression or punch line.

Clarence occasionally worked on numbers for other Motown artists, and Stevie and I often contributed. Stumped on a tune he was doing for the Supremes, called *Baby Doll*, Clarence gave it to me and said, "See what you can do."

I went down to the Star Waffle Shop that weekend, and over breakfast and about a dozen cups of coffee, wrote a new musical bridge. When I sang it to him on Monday, Clarence thought it was fantastic. "Boy, changing key in the bridge is just something that's never happened before! This is going to blow their minds!"

Unfortunately, that didn't happen. Holland Dozier and Holland had a string of hits with the Supremes at that time. Under Motown's method, a successful team of artists and writers was sacred. Other songwriters and produces never really had a chance getting their work released as singles because it might spoil the group's magic. Although *Baby Doll* never came out as a single, Clarence, Stevie and I received songwriter credit when it was included on *Supremes Sing Country Western & Pop*, an album Clarence produced in 1965.

I wrote several songs that were recorded but never released, including *Wedding Bells* and *Merry-go-round*, with Martha and the Vandellas singing backup for Stevie. But two of my songs were released, and both became regional hits in the northeast.

The first came out in the summer of '65. *Music Talk*, credited to Hull, Paul and Wonder, was the B side of Stevie's cover of *High Heel Sneakers*.

Music Talk had the newness Motown sought. It resulted from a conversation Stevie and I had on the bus in England. We were talking about how the English language seemed, in many ways, to be the worldwide language. Air traffic controllers and international pilots communicated in it. Every major foreign country had English-language newspaper editions. It was taught in virtually all schools around the world and was even required for students in Soviet Russia. Yet that didn't mean people everywhere spoke it. I made the remark that, actually, music is the only real international language. That stuck with me, and the lyrics to *Music Talk* started to take form:

> *The language of music is known*
> *Around the world.*
> *It's a language that's understood*
> *by people everywhere ...*

... If you're feelin'
What you're hearin'
Well don't you know
It's just the music, that pretty little music
Talkin' to your soul ....

When we checked into a hotel, I went up on the roof with a note pad and finished the lyrics. After getting back to Detroit, I set down the song's tune at the piano in my living room, then both Clarence and Stevie contributed their own creativity before it was recorded and released.

I enjoyed any time I could spend composing at my piano. Unfortunately, my neighbors didn't take as much pleasure from it as I did. The Chatham Apartments, where I was living then, was also home to another Motown member—Ron Miller, who was the only white songwriter I ever knew there. I asked him one day if our neighbors complained about his piano playing. Ron was puzzled. He'd had no complaints at all. I, on the other hand, got them all the time. Maybe it had something to do with the difference in our work. The songs he was writing are now among the great standards: *For Once In My Life*; *A Place In The Sun*; *Yester-Me, Yester-You, Yesterday*.

Neither *High Heel Sneakers* nor *Music Talk* were chart toppers, but my number did get re-recorded later by a female singer in England. It still must be floating around out there, because every once in a while a small royalty check from it shows up in my mail box.

The most successful tune I wrote came out the following December, as the flip side of Stevie's chart-topper *Uptight (Everything's Alright)*.

I'd written *Purple Raindrops* while in college, and did both the tune and lyrics in about fifteen minutes one Saturday morning. It was a tape of that number I'd first given Clarence when he asked to hear some of my work. When Stevie recorded it, I was naturally proud of the song and wanted only my name on it. What I didn't know then was that it was customary to share credit with anyone helped get a piece produced. It was a lesson I learned the hard way.

Before Stevie recorded *Purple Raindrops*, Clarence wanted me to write one more bridge to it, which I did. When the song came out, I discovered Clarence got one-third of the royalties and had his name on it as co-writer—I guess because he had suggested I change the tune slightly. As producer, I knew that Clarence would receive a commission, but his getting credit and a cut came as a surprise. No one had discussed such an arrangement with me.

No one told me, either, that other producers expected part of the action, too. Clarence had produced my number, but Mickey Stevenson was the producer on the A side, *Uptight (Everything's Alright)*. One day on the way to the airport with Mickey and his wife, Kim Weston, he said, "I understand you're getting a free ride on the flip side of my record."

From the tone of his voice, I sensed that, because I hadn't played by the unwritten rules. it wouldn't be easy for me to get another song released. And, in fact, I never did. When the album *Uptight (Everything's Alright)* came out, *Music Talk* was on it, but *Purple Raindrops* wasn't, even though it had been the more popular number. Looking back now, I wouldn't care how many names were added to mine on the label, or who got a kickback.

My naiveté might also have cost me another way, too. Christmas was the time for annual bonuses. After our final holiday show at the Fox that year, Rebecca Giles passed out large envelopes to everyone. Inside mine was only a letter from Gordy wishing me a merry Christmas. I doubt I was the only one who found nothing more, but it was a big disappointment as I watched others around me reacting happily to their checks. Even fifty bucks would have been a gratifying acknowledgment of my hard work with Stevie and my contribution to the company.

Motown's studio musicians were paid salary, but standard operating procedure was to share royalties with any contributing writer no matter how minor their participation. Even Lula received occasional writing credit. But in one instance a very deserving writer, Beans Bowles, was denied income he should have received. And in Beans' case, it was on the song that made "Little Stevie Wonder" famous.

Although he was a musician, Beans' job was technically management, a salaried position. When Clarence Paul and Hank Cosby

159

were writing *Fingertips*, Beans was the one who added the melody line. Rightfully, Beans wanted his share of any income the song might generate. He wasn't asking for credit on the label, just a usual piece of the action.

"They screwed me because I was in management and publishing was on the other side of a three-foot high divider across from me." There was no anger in his voice, just resignation. "I kept asking and they'd say, 'We don't have the papers ready.' Then it was, 'Two or three days.' The minute I went out of town, they signed the papers. When I came back, Clarence and Hank said, 'Don't worry about it. We'll give you some money.' Next thing, Clarence gets a new car and tells me, 'Damn, I forgot. I'll give you some money next time.' Stevie said he'd give me some money. Ha. He was only twelve. He didn't have any, and he didn't have enough control to give me any money. I have yet to get one penny from *Fingertips*."

Still, when it came to song writing, I was less interested in the money than in the thrill. I remember walking along a block in Philadelphia and hearing *Purple Raindrops* wafting onto the street from juke boxes in bars. A few days later in New York we had an afternoon engagement for Stevie to lip synch a couple of songs at a teenage dance in Harlem. When we walked in, *Purple Raindrops* was playing. There must have been a thousand kids there and they were all singing my song while they danced to it. I was floating!

That night at the Apollo, the audience began shouting for Stevie to do *Purple Raindrops*. Standing backstage, my pulse raced. Almost always, Stevie quickly launched into requests. But this time, he did something unusual.

"Who'd rather hear *With A Child's Heart*?" he asked. "How many want to hear *Purple Raindrops* and who wants to hear *With A Child's Heart*?"

That song had recently come out on flip side of *Nothing's Too Good For My Baby*. I'll be honest that applause was fairly equal in favor of either song. But my feelings were deeply hurt. Never before had I seen Stevie try to change an audience's request.

With A Child's Heart was written by Vicky Basemore. She was a sharp and very sexy young woman who lived in New York City. But she wasn't even at the show that night. If she had been, I'd have figured Stevie was out to impress her. (For that matter, so was I. I'd made a fairly serious play for her myself until Clarence let me know they had a pretty hot relationship. He may have been bluffing, but it worked. I backed off.)

Stevie sang *With a Child's Heart.* That he knew I was listening really hurt. He could be resentful of the control I had in his life, and I still believe he did it just to show me who was really in charge. But I never said a thing to him. I just let it go.

(Years later, it was a thrill to discover that *Purple Raindrops* still attracted attention. Felix Hernandez, a top DJ who's "Rhythm Revue" was named Best Radio Program of 1997 by *New York Magazine,* includes it in his list of the Top Ten B-Side R&B cuts.)

There were occasions, though, when I didn't ignore Stevie pulling rank as a star. I didn't like people treating Stevie as if he were so special that the rules were different for him. It was unhealthy, and I was the one who usually had to remind him of that.

On one occasion, Stevie, Ardena Johnston and I were in the car with Taylor Cox. The radio was on while we chatted. "Turn it off." Stevie interrupted our conversation. "I want to work on a song."

Taylor, who was driving, immediately reached for the knob. I put my arm out and stopped him.

"No, Stevie. You're one of four people here. We'd like to listen to the radio. You can't just tell us what to do and when to do it."

"Why not?" Taylor couldn't believe he'd heard me right. "This is what he does."

"Taylor," I said, "there's a time and a place for everything, even if you are Stevie Wonder."

"Yeah, I guess you're right," Taylor agreed.

Stevie wasn't happy with me, but I knew it was the right thing for me to do. Too often, people treated Stevie as someone special. And he really was, but I didn't want him to grow up blinded by his own glory. It was neither polite nor healthy for him to believe that everyone else should kowtow to his whims.

* * *

As much as I liked Clarence and understood his impact on Stevie's creative development, there were a lot of things that, morally, I didn't appreciate about him. Neither did Esther or Lula, and he was eventually removed as Stevie's musical director.

Esther and I never really saw eye to eye on Clarence. "You know why he and Stevie get along so well, don't you?" she said to me one day. "They're both fourteen-year-olds, and Clarence is the one who's never going to grow up."

Her derisive comment gave me a second of worry—since I considered Clarence a good friend, I wondered what she thought of me!

Clarence was no saint, but I felt his creative impact on Stevie was more important than his faults. Clarence loved Stevie with a strong brotherly affection and I knew would never intentionally be a bad influence. Years later I learned that if he had booze or pot around and Stevie would ask, "What's this?", Clarence didn't hesitate to say, "This isn't for you. I want you to keep clean."

Still, while Clarence could be creative, kind and considerate, he could also be incredibly self-centered and exactly the type of person I wanted to shield Stevie from. While I trusted Clarence, I never was completely comfortable leaving Stevie alone with him too long when we weren't working.

On some tours Stevie and I would ride with Clarence in his huge Chrysler Imperial instead of going on the bus or by plane. Being a serious drinker, Clarence didn't believe driving should keep him from the liquor. He carried a leather drinking pouch which he'd hold at arm's length, squirting wine into his mouth while tearing down the road. He controlled it enough to stay relatively sober at the wheel, though.

When he wasn't driving, it was a different story. Clarence would get flat-out drunk whenever he had the chance. It didn't matter whether or not there was a show to do. The biggest trouble was that he'd mix booze and pot, a combination packing more punch than any moonshine my relatives had ever brewed.

While there never was a time when he was too intoxicated to go on stage, there were times I couldn't believe he actually made it. Before one show in Washington, D.C., I found him in bed so plastered that I couldn't even wake him. I called the promoter and between the two of us we got Clarence up and moving. Over the next two hours we poured coffee into him, hauled him around the room, shoved him in and out of the shower and hollered at him a lot. I was mad. Stevie's show couldn't be canceled and there was no one else to handle Clarence's job. He managed to pull himself out of the stupor long enough to perform. He looked as miserable as he must have felt, and was barely able to direct the band. The promoter was so relieved Clarence made it that he rewarded him—with a fifth of whiskey.

He was always chasing women, too, and just couldn't keep his thing in his pants. After a show at the Fort Worth civic center, Stevie, the band and I were all in one big dressing room. The door was open and several young women stood there, watching the guys change out of their stage clothes. Clarence had his shirt off, his belt and zipper undone, and an enormous rise showing under his white boxer shorts. He pretended not to notice the groupies in the hall, but he strutted that room like a stud, parading his manhood for those women at the door.

Around Stevie, Clarence toned down his usually foul language unless musicians spun him into a frustrated rage, which happened with great regularity. During a scaled down version of a Motown Revue in Philadelphia, Stevie was, as usual, the closing act for all three shows that day. The final show ran late and his fans were going wild, and Stevie added an encore.

In the middle of a beautiful rendition of Count Basie's *Satin Doll*, several guys in the band got up, packed their instruments and walked off. The audience was stunned, Stevie was devastated, and Clarence was livid. With his back turned to the audience, he started cursing the band. To make matters worse, some of the musicians argued back, claiming they'd been hired at union scale for a set number of hours and time was up. We got the curtain closed just as the promoter joined the ruckus, as riled up as Clarence. For a band to pull that was something I'd never seen before or since.

As Stevie's stardom grew, Motown became increasingly uncomfortable with Clarence's on-stage involvement. Since Clarence, as musical director, was in charge of that part of the operation, I paid it little attention. But he was slowly making himself part of a duet act with Stevie, right down to matching stage outfits.

Stevie as part of a duo was not in Motown's plans. Early in 1964, after a short road trip, Esther called me. "Ted, Clarence is done. We're assigning someone else as Stevie's musical director."

When she explained why, I was surprised. I'd had no inkling either she or Berry had become so dissatisfied. My immediate worry was the impact this would have on Stevie.

"Listen, why don't we sit down and discuss it?" I cautioned. "Why be so abrupt? Let's discuss it, because it's been going on for a while."

"Okay," Esther agreed. "Get Stevie and Clarence and bring them back to my office."

Trying to play the mediator, I opened the meeting by explaining we needed to discuss the problem of Clarence's increasing role in Stevie's performances. Only there was no discussion. As soon as I finished, Esther told Clarence he was out as Stevie's musical director. "Now, is there anything else you want to talk about?"

So much for "discussion" and "working things out," I thought.

Wade Marcus, who had no interest in song writing, was named our new musical director. Wade was really a nice guy. He was educated, rather quiet, sophisticated and straight laced, and an excellent arranger— one of his best pieces for Stevie was an outstanding rendition of *Moon River*. But I'd been right to worry about how the loss of Clarence's creative motivation would affect Stevie. The change quickly showed in the boy. Over the months, I became more and more concerned about his diminishing interest in his work. Finally, I knew what had to be done.

I called Esther. "Wade's just not working out. We want Clarence back."

"You know what you're getting into," she argued, reminding me about Clarence's drinking, carousing and cursing. But she gave in. Clarence re-joined the "team" and Stevie's enthusiasm returned.

Less than two years later, though, Clarence was out for good. Gordy called him into his office one morning and, with no warning, announced, "You don't go back out with Stevie any more."

When Clarence asked why, Berry told him, "Lula doesn't want you on the road with him. She heard you swung a stick at him."

"I didn't even say nothing," Clarence told me, "'cause I said 'Who'd ever believe that? They got to be out of their minds.' I knew there wasn't no sense even arguing because it was so stupid. I told Berry, 'Berry, knowing Stevie, if I'da slung a stick at him, he woulda ducked.'"

I was disappointed to learn who'd supposedly started that rumor. Beau Bohannon, of all people, bragged it was he who cost Clarence his job. I knew Beau drove Clarence to distraction because he couldn't keep tempo with his left foot. "I'd start a tune in one tempo," Clarence said, "and get half way and that boy'd start slowing down to a waltz."

* * *

Behind-the-scenes issues like that were never allowed to affect Stevie's public appearances. But other trouble did. Too often, we'd show up for a gig only to find the piano out of tune or musicians who couldn't read music.

For years, finding musicians who could read music was a constant frustration. In a news paper article one day, I read a quote from a guitar player. He'd been asked if he could read music. "Yeah," he said, "but not enough to hurt my playing."

Having to deal with too many musicians like him, I didn't think his joke was funny.

Stevie's arrangements weren't complicated but they did have to be followed. Audiences deserved to hear songs performed as they were recorded. When we'd get into a new city, we expected promoters to provide bands who could read. We didn't have time to teach musicians to play every number from memory. Yet all too often shows would loom with unprepared bands. It was an ongoing worry I had to deal with. What would we do now? Bring in a whole new band? And if so, where in the world was I going to find them on such short notice?

A show at the Oakland City Auditorium in 1965 remains one of my most horrible memories. The band couldn't read a note. Making matters even worse, the promoter hadn't done his job well at all. In an auditorium that seated at least 2,000, there were less than a handful of people. We faced every performer's nightmare—a band that couldn't play the music, and no audience.

Clarence tried his best to teach the band. He finally gave up. "We just can't do this show," he admitted.

I told the promoter there was no way Stevie was going to perform. He argued that the musicians *could* play and claimed we were backing out because of the audience. That wasn't true. If there'd been only one person out there, Stevie would have performed as if it were a packed house. The fact of the matter was, the musicians simply couldn't do their jobs, which meant Stevie couldn't do his.

We flew home to Detroit. The promoter called me, threatening to sue Motown for breach of contract. I didn't think he had much of a case, but didn't look forward to the time, energy and money a lawsuit would consume. Then Clarence proposed the perfect solution.

I called the promoter back as Clarence suggested. "Tell you what," I offered. "Let's take this to court. You bring the band in and we'll bring our music. We'll see if your musicians can play it in front of the judge and jury."

That was the end of that.

Everywhere, people besieged us with pleas to listen to them play or hear a song they'd written. Brushing them off was a delicate act. Nearly all were untalented, but we wanted to stay open to those who were. Motown had found some excellent talent through unusual circumstances—Mickey Stevenson met songwriter Ron Miller when he delivered a pizza to Mickey's Chicago hotel room. Because we never knew what talent we'd encounter, or when we might need it, Clarence and I tried to be nice to such hopefuls.

When we flew into Richmond, Virginia, for a nightclub appearance in 1966, a baggage handler recognized Stevie. As we left the airport, he maneuvered a chance to talk to Clarence.

"Here's my phone number," the young man said. "If you ever need a band, you let me know 'cause I've got a good band!"

Clarence nodded politely and took the slip of paper the young man held out.

Well, we got to the club and here we go again—the house band couldn't read the music and had never played Stevie's tunes before. Clarence worked with them for about two hours before quitting in frustration.

"Well, hell," he finally said. "I'm gonna call that red cap. If only one guy in the band can read music, they've got to be better than what we got now."

In no time flat the red cap and his five friends arrived to live every amateur musician's dream. Whether they could read music or not never mattered, because they knew Stevie's music inside and out. As a group, they were good enough to have made it at Motown. They truly saved the show for us that night.

I complained for years about the problem of bad musicians, but it did no good. I finally reached the end of my patience in 1967. We were booked at a dump of a hall in Toledo—of course, there was no such thing then as a good place to do a show in Toledo. The neighborhood was bad, the show bill wasn't really strong, Stevie's time slot wasn't the best, and the whole thing was just no fun.

Road weary after traveling all night from another gig, Stevie, Beau and I arrived at the hall around five in the morning. Since we'd head home to Detroit as soon as Stevie finished the afternoon performance, we didn't check into a hotel. Hoping for a bit of rest in Stevie's dressing room backstage, we found Little Anthony asleep on top of the dresser. He'd spent the whole night there, since there was nowhere else to lay down.

Little Anthony and the Imperials were on the bill with Stevie. So was Solomon "Sonny" Burke. Sonny had started out as a child preacher in the early '40s, then became a gospel singer and a key figure behind bringing rhythm and blues into the music mainstream.

Sonny's band was supposed to back Stevie. Since we didn't have a musical director with us, Beau was in charge of rehearsal. The first thing he discovered was that none of them could read Stevie's music. I was pooped, perplexed and peeved no end when he told me. We were stuck with the band and had to make the show work somehow, I told Beau.

Word got back to Sonny that I was not happy, and he came looking for me back stage.

"Hey, I hear you're not satisfied with my band. As far as I'm concerned, you can do whatever you have to. You can call in the Toledo Orchestra if you want to."

I figured he was trying to lighten the situation with a joke. "That's a darned good idea," I joshed back. "I think I'll call them. Maybe I can get the Cleveland Orchestra, too."

Sonny exploded. This guy who'd headed a church at the age of thirteen cursed me up one side, down the other and back up again. I was so surprised I didn't say a word. Beau and Stevie did nothing to help the situation, either. Sitting nearby on a big trunk, they giggled like immature little kids the whole time. That only irritated me more and fueled Sonny's wrath.

During the show, Stevie worked with Solomon's band as best he could. After only three or four numbers he cut his performance short. His frustration only increased my anger over the situation. I swore he'd never be put in such a position again while I was around.

Considering how much I'd complained about the problem over the years, I wasn't sure what I could do to actually get it resolved. I'd talked to people at Motown till I was blue in the face and it hadn't done any good. I couldn't get in to see Berry. I decided the only thing left to do was put my complaint in writing.

In a letter to Berry I laid out page after page of episodes where the bands couldn't read music, musicians who didn't show, pianos that weren't tuned, and every other thing that made it almost impossible for Stevie to do a decent show. I told Berry I'd made three appointments with him to discuss the problem, that I'd come to the office each time from the School for the Blind in Lansing only to be told he couldn't see me because of important business. It was about time, I stated, that he realized this was pretty important business, too. And I was resentful of the fact that these problems hadn't been resolved.

The letter did the trick. Word quickly came back to me Berry would handle it. He immediately implemented new clauses in everyone's show contracts requiring promoters to provide tuned pianos and properly functioning sound systems. Motown also set up a network of key people in each city who would ensure quality musicians for all the shows. Never again would Stevie or I have to deal with frustrations that should never have occurred in the first place.

* * *

I wasn't the only one frustrated by Motown's seeming lack of interest in support of Stevie. By the time he was sixteen, he had learned so much that, in many ways, he was already a mature musician. Yet because he was young, a lot of people found it hard to accept the growth of his talent. When he tried to contribute creatively, he'd be brushed off by those who couldn't see beyond Little" Stevie. I'd step in as his advocate, reminding the writers and producers that he could do more than they were letting him, and that Stevie's ideas deserved to be heard. Unfortunately, they turned a deaf ear to me as well as to Stevie, and his disillusionment with Motown grew.

One day while doing class work at my apartment, a song by The Steam (who later hit No. 1 with *Na Na Na Na, Hey, Hey, Hey, Good-bye*) came on the radio. Although their sound was very different from Motown's, Stevie and the lead singer's voice had a similarity.

"Boy, that sounds like you," I said, "and that's a really good song."

"Yeah," he sighed. "You know, that's the kind of stuff I ought to be allowed to do."

Clarence had encouraged Stevie's creativity and school exposed him to finer points that also inspired his talent. The musical education he received at the School for the Blind was outstanding. For fewer than three hundred students, there were five faculty on the music staff alone.

At no other public school in Michigan did every student study orchestra, piano and voice on a daily basis. Along with his private piano lessons, Stevie learned to play both string bass and violin. He learned music composition and chord structure, and was trained in classical music.

Everything Stevie learned fostered his genius, but no one at Motown seemed to care. Until one winter day in his senior year at the School for the Blind, when Stevie's frustration erupted in a burst of creative energy. It was typical of him to use his piano period to mess around writing songs. That day he wrote an entire number in the one-hour period.

This time, Stevie wasn't going to be ignored by Motown. When he insisted that his song be heard, Gordy admitted the number had "a little potential." He gave it to Sylvia Moy and Hank Cosby for a bit of final polish.

Stevie's song was produced as the B side of a single called *I Don't Know Why*. That number never even made it into the Top 40. *My Cherie Amour*, the first song concept credited to Stevie, shot into the Top Five. And remains, to this day, one of his greatest hits.

* * *

A few months before he graduated high school in 1969, a group of us were in Washington, D.C. for a ceremony honoring Stevie. Afterward, we held an impromptu celebration in Stevie's hotel room. Stevie was playing an electric piano, an instrument that had just been introduced.

There was a knock at the door and my friend Gordon Steinhauer answered it.

"Sir," a bellhop admonished, "we've had several complaints about the noise from guests on this floor. This is a conservative hotel and I'll have to ask you to keep it down."

"I'm sorry," Gordon immediately apologized. "But this is Stevie Wonder and we're sort of celebrating. But we'll keep it down. Tell the guests we're sorry."

Five minutes later, there was another knock at the door. Gordon answered it again. Again it was the bellhop again.

"Look," Gordon said, "we turned down the music and we're trying to be quiet. What's the problem now?"

This time the bellhop smiled. "Sir, I went up and down the hall and I told everybody it was Stevie Wonder and a celebration and they all said that it's okay. They also asked, could you leave the door open, so they can hear better?"

As our party continued, I recalled the days when Ron Miller and I had lived in the same apartment building. Funny, I thought, how who's doing the playing makes all the difference.

Be Cool, Be Calm

*"The only people who are really blind are those whose eyes
are so obscured by hatred and bigotry that they can't see
the light of love and justice."*

— *Stevie Wonder*

Stevie and I were color blind to a great extent. We didn't notice a lot
of racial things simply because we couldn't see them. Plus, with our
attitudes, our natures, we weren't constantly on the lookout for it. But no
one in the 1960s was immune to the racially and politically charged
times we lived in. And I know my perspective was unique.

I'll never forget my first introduction to the Motown entourage, at
the Howard Theater in Washington, D.C. "I'd like you to meet Stevie's
new tutor," Esther Edwards said as she gestured my way. "He's that
colored fellow over there." All of us laughed, and it was our senses of
humor that got us through many tense times.

Whites were most definitely the minority in Motown, certainly not
through any overt, negative bias. Whenever possible, the Gordy's hired
blacks, often giving people an opportunity to improve themselves. But
when it came right down to it, Berry insisted on the best people for the
jobs. And if that meant a white man, that was fine. Because everyone at
Motown knew there was only one truly universal color: green. As in
money.

Barney Ales and Ron Miller are the only other white people I
remember during my years in Motown. But as the only teacher in the
company, I was literally a minority of one. Since I spent virtually all of
my time working with Stevie and the few who had a direct role in his

172

career, I was doubly insulated from most of the Motown staff. Adding a third layer of distance was my very poor vision.

I was always very much at ease with Esther and Berry, Beans, Clarence, Gene Shelby and the others in our small crowd. There were a lot of nice people at the office but, because I hardly knew them, I was always self-conscious around them. One of the worst parties I've ever been to was a company Christmas party my wife and I attended. Everybody ignored us. It was embarrassing. But looking back, I must have seemed aloof to those who didn't know me well. I've learned to compensate so well for my poor eyesight that most people don't realize I don't see them. They think I'm ignoring them, when actually I'm completely unaware unless they're standing very near me. Compounding the problem is that I can recognize white faces better than dark. Identifying the faces of black people I don't know well has always been difficult. I'm sure if my vision were better, I'd notice people more quickly, be more aggressive in approaching them and put them at ease. It's a social problem that people with vision impairments struggle with constantly.

I knew jokes were cracked about me. Beau and Stevie often called me "The Man"—which definitely meant "the *white* man", and that some people would have preferred a black man in my job. The fact was, there wasn't a black man in Michigan then who taught the blind. There were only two black staff members at the School for the Blind, and both were women—one was a teacher, the other, my darling friend Marie Paz, a nurse.

"But everybody respected you," Gene Shelby told me, "because they found out what Stevie was learning, and he could spell and read better than some of them."

Only Martha Reeves clearly let it be known she resented my white presence in a black organization. On one of my rare evenings out without Stevie, Taylor Cox and I went to hear Wilson Picket at the Twenty Grand, then an excellent black nightclub in Detroit. People who knew Taylor stopped at the bar, greeted him and were polite to me. Once in a while was I aware of a cold shoulder, but not from people who knew me.

I wasn't uncomfortable. Until Martha, taking a seat next to Taylor, loudly sneered, "What's *he* doing here?"

Taylor was one of the few people at Motown with whom I socialized. I was careful to maintain some distance with key players in the company, aware that personal relationships could lead to conflicts of interest, or at least create that perception. And the last thing I wanted to do was fall in love with someone at Motown, which would have complicated both my job and my life.

I could easily have let it happen. Diana Ross was certainly of prime interest. She was always so charming and flirty with me. Tammy Terrell, as sweet and friendly as she was pretty, loved my song *Purple Raindrops* and wanted me to write one for her. There were others, but constant travel and having Stevie always at my side made any social life difficult.

My being white and these women being black did enter my mind. I had no problem with that, but I knew others would. Even my own parents, who were not bigoted, would have had difficulty accepting such a relationship no matter what they said.

My mother was extremely proud of my role in Stevie's life and proud that, as a Southerner, she'd raised me to be unprejudiced. To this day, I clearly recall my first experience with racial inequality.

It was in Chattanooga. I was eight or nine years old and riding the bus downtown to pay some family bills. My mother had definitely drummed proper bus etiquette into me: a gentleman always offered his seat to a lady. When a black woman boarded and stood in the aisle, I got up. "You may have my seat, ma'am," I politely offered. When she refused, I was embarrassed.

At home, I told my mother and asked what I had done wrong. Nothing, she explained—Negroes could sit only at the back of the bus, and under no circumstances could they ever accept a seat from a white person. What she couldn't help me understand was why.

I didn't realize until much later that, even in the people I loved, beliefs and unconscious feelings might be two very different things. One warm summer night, I took Stevie with me to my folk's house in Lansing. The whole family was partying around the backyard pool when we arrived. But after Stevie jumped in, I noticed that slowly and one by

174

one, everyone else got out. Unsure whether the others got out because Stevie was black, because they felt self-conscious around someone so famous, or because he was blind, I was embarrassed. I realized they were completely unaware of the message their actions sent. I got in the pool with Stevie, but no one else joined us.

I never got used to people who, on the surface, could admire Stevie for his talent but still not accept him because he was black. To think that it was possible in my own family was especially disconcerting.

The Michigan School for the Blind was a particularly protective environment in an otherwise racially turbulent world. Out of the three hundred or so students, Stevie, his best friend J.J. Jackson and J.J.'s brother Milton made up about a third of the black students. Much like musicians, the kids at school responded to goodness and ability, not color. Campus was a cocoon with no room for racism or prejudice. But even it wasn't totally insulated.

It was Michigan's turn to host the Eastern wrestling championship for schools for the blind in 1966. An annual event, the meet also drew coaches and superintendents from outside the region. The superintendent of the host school, as Dr. Thompson muttered, "got stuck having to entertain people."

Dr. Thompson always made it clear the school was not to "use" its famous student, but after careful consideration he invited Stevie to perform before the dinner party at his home. "I asked Stevie if he'd give us a few minutes of music a la Motown and he said he would. I think he took my request in the same spirit as if I'd asked one of the wrestlers to demonstrate a new hold nobody else had. Stevie did a superb job."

Unfortunately, pride in his student's talent turned to dismay with one of his fellow superintendents, though. Dr. Thompson remembered one superintendent of a Southern school didn't like the idea of a black adolescent entertaining white adults. "But then, he was a little short of appreciation of talent. Four or five beers later he might have been softened up a little bit, but that was a disappointment."

Only once did I encounter a negative racial comment about Stevie at school. I was standing at the administration building doorway, as I often did, watching for him after the lunch break on day in 1968. A dean of students, whom I'd always thought was a terrific fellow, stood nearby when Stevie walked past. Dressed very differently than his conservative, blue-collar-family classmates, he wore a brightly colored African-style dashiki, a loose fitting shirt very popular then.

The dean was taken aback. "Boy, Stevie's really going back to his roots."

His voice made it clear he was offended by Stevie's appearance. I sighed, but said nothing, knowing that so many of the changes white people were seeing in blacks were somewhat frightening and hard to understand.

* * *

Like me, most of the black people at Motown had their roots in the South. Several, such as Stevie's mom, Clarence Paul, Shorty Long and Otis Williams, came to Detroit as young adults. Others, like Diana Ross, were born after their parents came North during World War II, often for factory jobs.

Northern whites, especially during the '60s, tended to consider themselves "superior" to Southern whites on racial issues. But they weren't different in their prejudices—just in the way they expressed them. Too often, I recognized, Northerners respected blacks as a race but wanted nothing to do with them as individuals. In the South, it seemed the opposite. Some whites could care deeply about the black individuals who were part of their lives, yet remain staunchly opposed to racial equality.

Most of the Motown Revues played down South. It was where our strength was in record sales and recognition. And the tours were popular with many of the artists. I often heard, "Down South I know where I stand. Up North here, they don't tell you."

All of us were naive enough to think things should be different. Only weeks before the second Motown Revue, President Lyndon Johnson had signed the Civil Rights Act of 1964 into law, "eliminating the last vestiges of discrimination," as the press reported. Things were supposed to be better for everyone. Besides, the Motown artists were famous stars, important in the music industry and to their fans. But what the law said and how whites felt were two very different things. If your skin was black, bigots didn't give a hoot if your name was Marvin Gaye, Diana Ross or Stevie Wonder.

On the Revue in 1964, I quickly discovered how blatant discrimination could be. At a restaurant in Georgia, someone went inside to let them know we had a bus full of people hungry for lunch. Word came that everyone was welcome—around back in the kitchen. A joke was made that I could eat in the restaurant if I wanted.

Cynical humor covered much of our anger over such treatment, and my bus-mates enjoyed seeing how I'd react to such first-hand treatment. I handled it like they did, accepting the fact that this was how it was but not liking it one bit. We all walked around to the kitchen, got our lunches and ate them on the bus.

Another time, just after passing a sign proclaiming "Martin Luther King is a Communist," we stopped at a restaurant crowded with lunch diners, only to see a white face hastily pull down the window shades and stick the "Closed" sign on the door. At times like that, it wasn't easy for me to remain philosophical or lighthearted with Stevie.

Stopping during the day might be uncomfortable, but after dark, we knew things could get downright dangerous. On the 1963 Motown Revue, shots had been fired at the bus after the Birmingham, Alabama show. It was bad enough for blacks, but adding a white face to the group only compounded problems. White Freedom Riders from the North were particularly reviled throughout the South, often beaten and occasionally murdered. In fact, shortly before the 1964 Motown Revue, three young Freedom Riders—two white men and a black man, disappeared in Mississippi. Our tour was long over before their bodies were found.

During the summer of 1966, Stevie and I drove part of the tour with Clarence, instead of riding on the bus. Along with us was Joe Thomas, who was in his early 20's and working as Stevie's valet. Dusk was falling, and after a day on the road, we were hungry. On the outskirts of a small Georgia town, Clarence pulled his big black Chrysler into a drive-in. All the faces in the cars around us were white. I could feel the question hanging in the air: What were these three black guys up to, and how come a white guy was with them?

Racial tension was high all across the country. I was apprehensive, concerned about what they were thinking and what they might do. I reached for the set of bongos we had in the car and put them on the dashboard. I figured it was the quickest, most obvious way to settle any questions about who we were. Clarence understood, but Joe's let out a hoot of derisive laughter. "Oooh, I think Teddy's scared."

Damned right!, I thought, Ted's real nervous because Ted wouldn't be the first white guy to take a bullet down South. And get his black friends killed along with him.

But we tried to pull humor out of situations whenever we could. Finding public facilities was almost as much a problem as finding places to eat. On the way out of Atlanta after a gig at the Peacock Lounge, Stevie asked Clarence to find a restroom. Stopping at the next service station, Clarence said, "Come on, man, I'll take you."

Typical of the times, the gas station's bathrooms were segregated. Clarence steered Stevie through the "whites only" door and waited. As they walked back to the car, the attendant ran out the station door, sputtering in rage.

"Hey, man! Can't you see the sign? You can't ... You not supposed to take ... You're not supposed to use that bathroom!"

"I didn't." Clarence's voice was pleasant and they kept moving. "He did. Besides, man, he's blind."

"Well, *you're* not blind," the attendant snapped.

Clarence opened the car door and Stevie got in. "Yeah, but, man, I didn't have to pee, either."

Segregated facilities presented a bit of a dilemma for me. Stevie and I were out for a walk one day in Tennessee when we decided to stop at a Dairy Queen. "You're not going to believe this," I told Stevie. "They still have separate windows for coloreds and whites."

"Which one are we going to?" Stevie asked.

"Since I'm paying, we *both* go to the white's," I said.

Finding decent food and lodging were our two most important concerns on the road. Motown always made our room reservations before we left Detroit. Often, though, the hotel management wouldn't know until we showed up that forty-nine out of the fifty of us were black. On more than one occasion I went in first to let them know make sure the reservations were in order and just generally break the ice. I appreciated that Berry or Esther, or whoever had first suggested it, had confidence I had the right attitude to handle what could be a delicate situation. The concern was that if our entire group walked in together, we'd be told, "No, we don't have any reservations. You can't stay here."

Only once, in Virginia, did a hotel owner try to turn us away. I immediately realized it had nothing to do with his personal prejudice and everything to do with fear. And I understood why. While we'd be leaving the next day, his livelihood could be seriously threatened by his neighbors and the community. We reached a compromise with the help of another hotel: our room reservations would be honored if we'd agree to eat at the hotel across the street. It was a way of sharing the responsibility and reducing local tension.

We agreed. We hadn't planned to eat at our hotel anyway. Most of the Motown musicians had played in these towns before. They knew where the black restaurants were, where we'd be accepted and could get good soul food. Those were the places we wanted to go.

The only time we stayed at a black-operated hotel was an embarrassment to us all. As far as I can recall, Chattanooga was the only town we ever played where Motown found a black-owned establishment and saw an opportunity to support another black business. Unfortunately, the hotel didn't deserve anybody's business. It was a dump. The rooms were filthy, the linens dingy, everything was run down. I could tell Berry was unhappy with the situation, but by then we had no other choice. I was chagrined that my friends were getting a poor impression of the city I remembered so fondly from my childhood. What almost made up for our lousy accommodations was the fantastic reception we got from the mostly white audience at our show.

Many a time we'd arrive in a new city for a gig and have no idea where we'd be appearing. Especially in the early years, it was usually in the black part of town. We'd find the right area, stop somebody on the street and ask, "Where's the dance?" Everybody would know where the dance was being held, and that's where our show would be.

In those days, the Revues played some real bad places, often stark armories with terrible acoustics, in neighborhoods where white people were afraid to go, especially after dark. And more than once during a show a gun shot or two would ring out. The band and all the artists would dive for backstage. Sometimes, after order was restored, the show would go on. Usually, though, it was two-thirds over by the time some guy got drunk enough to make a pass at someone else's girl. We'd just wait for the cops to arrive and clear out the crowd, then get back on the bus and take quiet leave.

A lot of people in Motown, like the Four Tops and the Temptations, carried guns. I never encountered any incident that caused me to consider such self-protection. What amazes me now is that I used to walk around with several thousand dollars in my pockets all the time. I couldn't leave the money in the hotel room, so I'd just carry it in my sport coat or briefcase, even when I went walking around Philadelphia's Uptown Theater or the Apollo in Harlem. While theater lights made those areas seem glamorous at night, in daylight these were unquestionably drug infested ghettos. Cops would've thought I was crazy, a white guy confidently carrying so much cash. I think the reason I never had a problem is people probably figured I was an undercover officer myself. I just went any place I wanted, without fear. Now, I wonder whether it was confidence or sheer stupidity.

*   *   *

Looking back, I recognize several situations that were more racially charged than I thought at the time. As a white man, I hadn't grown up experiencing discrimination, so it wasn't constantly on my mind. I didn't see the people I worked with as black. I saw them as my friends. Of course, I couldn't see much at all. But sometimes the discrimination hit—literally. And it was often directed at me, I guess because I was a safer target.

Stevie and I were walking down Sunset Boulevard one afternoon when a very large white man slammed his shoulder into me, nearly knocking me from my feet. He kept right on going, no apology, no nothing. My first reaction was naively charitable: "Well, the guy accidentally ran into me." Then I thought it over and realized he'd intentionally crossed the street for the express purpose of proving his bigotry.

Others were more subtle, and snide. Going through a cafeteria line in Ohio, one of the servers recognized Stevie. All the employees, both black and white, excitedly sought his autograph. One white fellow was particularly interested and spent a lot of time chatting with Stevie, obviously impressed. Then he turned to me. "Hey, aren't you the wrong color to be traveling with this group?"

On our first trip to London in 1963, Stevie and I met Del Shannon at the BBC, where both were scheduled on a radio interview show. Just a couple years younger than I, Del was from a small town outside of Grand Rapids, where I'd lived. Famous for his hit song *Runaway*, he was on tour promoting his newest record, *Little Town Flirt*. When we were introduced, Del enthusiastically greeted Stevie. But when I reached out to shake his hand, he turned away. Stevie enjoyed a lively and pleasant conversation with the singer, while the cold looks I got carried a much less-pleasant message. Del gave me the distinct impression he didn't approve of a white man living and working so closely with blacks.

Whites didn't hold exclusive rights to bigotry, by any means. It was hurtful to be treated shabbily by some of the blacks who were so friendly to Stevie. He wasn't aware of the cold shoulders, cold looks and refused handshakes I encountered when we were together. I just had to stand there and put up with it. Most often I ignored it as part of the job, and didn't make an issue out of it with Stevie.

Sometimes, though, the two of us enjoyed turning the tables on bigots, leaving them as embarrassed as they deserved to be.

I hailed a taxi one night in Philadelphia. Stevie scooted in first, moving behind the cabby.

"Boy, I'll tell you It's a good thing you were under the light because I almost never stop for anybody in this neighborhood," the guy said, immediately setting himself up for a fall.

"Oh, is that right?" I asked.

"Yeah, the niggers around here, you can't trust 'em." His voice wasn't angry, just matter of fact.

I reached over and squeezed Stevie's arm, signaling him to stay quiet—we'd have some fun with this one. It was obvious he hadn't noticed Stevie. He'd only seen me, the white guy.

For the few minutes we were in the cab, the guy spewed all of his racial problems and views. He was still carrying on when we pulled up in front of our well lit hotel. Stevie and I got out and both of us leaned down at the window. The driver's face froze in shock.

"You know you don't deserve this," I stated as I paid our fare—plus an outrageously large tip. Then Stevie and I turned and walked away, laughing aloud at the fool he'd made of himself.

* * *

While personal sentiments at Motown definitely supported the civil rights movement and the company was quietly recording Martin Luther King's public speeches for posterity, the only "protest" numbers being released were lost-love songs like *The Tracks of My Tears*. Then in 1966, Clarence arranged a duet of *Blowin' in the Wind*. A spoken-word introduction I wrote for it gave Stevie his first opportunity to express his personal feelings. He loved doing that song and audiences loved hearing it, both for its political message and for the soulful blend of Stevie's and Clarence's voices. Stevie's cover of Bob Dylan's number reached No. 9 on the charts, but it would still be several more years before any other Motown release seriously touched on the racial issues of the day.

Yet in its own way, Motown had a dramatic impact on black-white relations. It was the first black music company to get crossover play on white radio stations. Of that fact, author Gerald Early wrote in *One Nation Under A Groove*, "It was quite possible, at last, to think of entering the world of whites without going through the back door of culture."

The civil rights movement focused on better treatment of blacks. And a natural, although disturbing, reaction on the part of many black people, especially the young, was to vent anger toward any white person they encountered. One morning in 1966 as we arrived before the show at the Steel Pier, several teenagers waited at the stage door. Stevie greeted them as we made our way past, but they wanted him to stay and chat. After a moment, I said, "I'm sorry, kids, we've really got to go."

In an instant the atmosphere snapped from fan adoration to fanatical anger. They began shoving at me, pulling on Stevie, becoming more and more menacing. With Stevie holding my elbow, I managed to push our way to safety behind the stage door. Stevie was shocked by their behavior, but what happened later at one of the shows was even more frightening.

It wasn't at all unusual for Stevie to introduce me to his audiences, since they'd often see me. In new settings we'd use the sighted guide technique to get him on and off stage. Occasionally I'd pop out to retrieve a flying drumstick or dropped harmonica. That night, at the end of the show, I went out to walk him off-stage. As Stevie introduced me, the crowd's murmur grew into an angry swell. People started rising from their seats. I had no idea what they might do, but I Knew they were angry. I left quickly. After a moment, the situation quieted enough for Stevie to do his planned encore. One of the black members of the crew guided him back to the dressing room, where I waited. Both of us were alarmed by the audience's reaction to me and didn't leave the theater until long after the crowd dispersed.

* * *

Only once did Stevie and I get into a serious argument about race, long before he saw first-hand that blacks could be as bigoted as whites. It was on our 1964 trip to Paris, during that period of Stevie's adolescence that was so trying for us both.

183

On a Greyline bus tour of the city, we talked about the international roster of acts he was appearing with at the Olympia, about how well everyone from all the different countries got along, and how there just seemed to be no racial discrimination in Paris. Neither of us understood why things couldn't be so easy back home in the states.

As dusk fell, the bus stopped on a hilltop overlooking the City of Lights and the passengers got out to enjoy the view. Sitting on the grass, still thinking about our conversation, I said, "You know, I think things really are getting better."

"Yeah, white folks like to think so." Stevie's voice carried a note of contempt. "All white people want to believe there aren't any problems. They want to believe it and they make themselves believe it. They're all the same."

"When you talk about 'all white people'," I snapped back, "you're talking about me. I'm not that way. And you're talking about the friends of mine you've gotten to know, and the teachers and kids at school. Saying 'all white people' is just as prejudiced as saying 'all blacks.' And I don't appreciate that negative attitude."

I continued to fume silently and Stevie was quiet for a moment. "I'm sorry. I know you're right. But I still think a lot of white people have their heads in the sand. Nothing's ever really going to change."

Now, thirty-some years later, I have to agree that, as much as things have changed on the surface, human fears and prejudices have changed so little. All any of us can do is make things better one person at a time— and it has to start within ourselves. I'm blessed to know that my role in Stevie's life, while we were both young and still hoped that all people could love one another, helped him grow up with an understanding of whites he might not have otherwise had.

When it came to Vietnam, though, we never saw eye to eye. We constantly debated U.S. involvement in the war. Older and more conservative, I was as confused as everyone else about why we were fighting, but I supported the government. I was dead set against the antiwar demonstrations, believing they only prolonged the fighting. Stevie related emotionally to the flower children of the '60s and their message, and always sided with the underdog. Though I never really gave in, I'll admit that as his reasoning skills developed and his arguments improved, what he said made me think more critically.

Still, I continued to remind him he shouldn't be giving advice to the world. I was, quite frankly, not impressed with sixteen- and seventeen-year-old prophets, and Stevie was beginning to feel he was one. I expected him to mature and have some education before spouting off about what people should believe. Now, he's a thoughtful spokesman whose wisdom, words and actions make me proud.

A lot of kids don't have much interest in philosophical discussions, but Stevie had a natural bent in that direction. We had Vietnam, we had riots, we had hippies and drugs. While I didn't always agree with how younger people were touting their messages, Stevie and I did agree it was time for love to replace hate.

If I can give Stevie any compliment, it is that he really had such a loving nature and wanted everyone to love him. But hatred and death shrouded the whole years. John F. Kennedy's assassination opened possibly the most turbulent and violent public period this nation has ever endured. Two years later, the murder of Malcolm X stunned the country. Whether blacks agreed with his philosophy was less important than the fact he was working to empower his race. The majority of whites, myself included, really knew little of the man or his work, other than the often-negative information supplied by an ambivalent media. The fact that his death came at the hands of his own people was especially painful for everyone interested in racial equality.

But the year that really brought us all to our knees was 1968. On a balmy April evening, the kind of glorious spring night that makes harsh Michigan winters seem so irrelevant, Stevie and I were riding back to Detroit from the School for the Blind. It had been a long week and I was ticked off at Gene Shelby for being an hour and a half late in picking us up. I was tired, I wanted to get home, grab a beer and relax with my wife.

Stevie and I were riding in the back seat, half dozing, when a bulletin burst from the radio, turning the night darker than blindness can ever cause: Martin Luther King had just been assassinated in Memphis, Tennessee.

With Stevie's compassionate nature, it was only natural he'd been drawn to Dr. King's dream. So was I, and I'd positively glowed when we met the great man in 1966, at the Student Christian Leadership Conference Freedom Rally in Chicago where Stevie appeared.

Gene clicked off the car radio. No one said a word. There were none to say, and our throats wouldn't have managed them if there were. Stevie reached over for my hand. And we held that clasp for the remainder of our silent journey.

I'd lost all interest in going out that night. As I lay in my darkened apartment a while later, the phone rang. It was Lula. We talked for a while, trying somehow to console each other. "They always shoot the good ones," she lamented.

That call from Lula was so important to me. Many blacks blamed any and every white person for every racial atrocity. After so many instances feeling Lula's distrust, her phone call told me what she didn't say in words—that my being white didn't make me responsible for the horror we were experiencing.

We thought we'd lived through the worst, but two months and two days later we discovered that even the worst could be compounded.

Stevie and I, with my wife Margaret, were in California. Arriving in Los Angeles, we felt so cool to find presidential candidate Robert Kennedy were staying in the same hotel. Bobby Kennedy had become the Great White Hope of our generation. Stevie and I were both disappointed that our schedule meant we'd miss attending any of his political rallies. We both envied Margaret when she got to shake Bobby's hand during a march along Hollywood Boulevard.

That night, after Stevie's show, pandemonium greeted us on our return to the Ambassador Hotel. Moments after leaving a primary election party in the ballroom, the second Kennedy brother was dead at the hand of an assassin.

Individuals weren't the only ones dying. Riots were killing our cities, murdering the souls of our communities. In the week following Dr. King's death, riots exploded in one hundred twenty-five cities. The summer of 1968 culminated a terrifying trend begun at Watts in 1965. For three "long, hot summers," as they were known, racial tension was the powder keg that sparked riots across our nation's alphabet. Baltimore. Birmingham. Chicago. Houston, Memphis. Nashville. Raleigh. Trenton. Washington DC.

And smack dab in the middle, in the summer of 1967, was Detroit.

My sister Joan, my wife Margaret and I were in Baltimore, where Stevie was doing a show with Ray Charles and Dionne Warwick—the first time they'd shared a bill since our 1963 trip to Paris. Stevie's shows, in a beautiful auditorium, were fabulous. Margaret and I had been married less than a month, so the trip a bit of a honeymoon. Stevie and Ardena Johnston stayed on in Baltimore when Margaret, my sister and I flew home in a high mood. At the Detroit airport, Margaret and I caught a cab to our apartment.

As the taxi neared the city, the scent and sight of black smoke filling the sky grew more and more menacing. Our driver didn't even comment, but finally, too curious to ignore it, I asked, "What's all the smoke from?"

"Well, yeah," he shrugged, "there's a lot of sirens going off."

"What do you mean?" Margaret pressed.

The driver's glance in the rearview mirror was surprised. "It's the riots. The whole city's burning. Didn't you know?"

We didn't. This was the middle of the week. The riot had started the previous Sunday, on July 23rd. There'd been no mention in any news we'd heard while out of town. Terror and fear now replaced our simple curiosity.

The Motown office sat in the heart of the riot center. Stevie's mother and family lived nearby on Greenlawn Street. The apartment Margaret and I had was only a dozen blocks away. Our panic grew as the cab made its way through the smoldering nightmare. We had no idea what we'd find at home, or if we'd even be safe getting there.

There was no question of the riot's severity, but it was public hysteria that really overwhelmed the city. Dusk-to-dawn curfews were in effect and nearly everything was shut down. For several days, no supermarkets were open, nor any other place to get food. Days later, on Saturday, Margaret and I heard a radio announcement that the nearby Food Liner on Woodward Avenue was open. By the time we got there, the store was packed. In a crowded aisle, a real large, healthy looking black man purposely shoved me. No way was I going to shove back, knowing the whole place could burst into violence. But most of the people—white and black alike—were just trying to get what supplies they could and hurry home.

Even home wasn't always safe. Across the street from our apartment was a dry cleaners, and the owner stayed around the clock to protect his property. Sure enough, one night a group of rioters tried to break in and loot. As shotgun blasts erupted out on the street, Margaret and I dove under the bed.

When the riots ended a week after they started, forty people had died—thirty-three of them black, seven white. Two thousand were injured and five thousand left homeless.

By the time things calmed down enough for the Motown office to re-open, we learned Hitsville hadn't escaped unscathed. A tank had fired across Grand Boulevard, sending a shell through a window and out the roof. And the stories we shared about our individual experiences during the riots made me realize how close I'd come to losing friends to the violence.

The whole mess had started on 12th Street, in the block where Earl Van Dyke and a few other Motown musicians were playing at the Chit Chat Club. Earl claimed the riot was set off by an after-hours police raid there. Members of the Detroit Police force, which was ninety percent white, were known to misuse their power and apparently did that night.

The blacks had finally had enough of the ill-treatment they were supposed to take whenever the police chose to dish it out. For example, any time they wanted, the cops could declare what was called "Operation Stress," where they'd send out a decoy as an extremely tempting robbery victim. It was a blatant entrapment ploy used only in the ghetto as a way to arrest blacks. Or the cops would declare curfews for black areas only. There was also a notorious crew in the department, known as the Big Four, who were flagrant about their racism. "They were like cowboys," Beans said. "They were quick draw artists. And they practiced on black people."

Later, talking about the riot, he recalled, "We were playing at the Fox Theater (on Woodward Avenue) that night and we were swinging like hell. It was an interracial band, an interracial show. Motown heavy. CKLW DJ Robin Seymour came out and stopped the show. He said, 'Ladies and gentlemen, don't panic, but Detroit's on fire. There's a mob marching down Woodward right now. We hope to get this thing over with and do this show again one day. But right now, the city of Detroit is in a turmoil and we want you all to go home safely.'"

Beans and his wife were divorced, and that night his two young sons were with him. He had to find a way to get them home. "As we drive down the freeway," he continued, "flames are shooting over the freeway from both sides. The damn place was on fire! I got my kids home, came back down to Motown for my things and got back to my apartment. The next night, I'm eating graham crackers and drinking milk. The National Guard had been called in. They'd cordoned off the streets. All the street lights have been burned out, knocked out or disrupted. I'm standing at the open window looking out—I was on the third floor—and see this Jeep pulling down the street. I hear gunshots and this spotlight shines in my face. A guy yells at me, 'What are you doing up there?'

"I tell him, 'Drinking milk and eating graham crackers.' 'You should get out of that window,' he says. 'It's kind of dangerous.' The spotlight went out, I looked down and this guy's got a cannon pointed at me! They were out looking for snipers."

A chill ran up my spine. Virtually the exact same thing had happened to me.

I'd been standing at the window of our fifth-floor apartment, looking out through binoculars, when a Jeep-load of guardsmen came around the corner. They shined a searchlight at me and one of them hollered, "You! What are you doing?"

"Just seeing what I can," I called back down.

"Get your head in!" another one of the shouted back.

Margaret looked out and quickly yanked me away. "Oh my God, Ted! They've got their guns pointed at you!"

But show business goes on. A few days later we were back on the road again.

The Lonesome Road

"As soon as Stevie's finished with school, Motown will drop Ted like a hot potato."
— Dr. Robert Thompson

Six years had passed since I'd become Stevie's teacher, and the whole world had changed so dramatically. Especially my world. I'd joined Motown when it was a small family operation. Now, it was a multi-million dollar company and the impact of its artists and music spanned the globe. I'd come to work with "Little Stevie Wonder," a skinny bundle of energy whose head barely reached my shoulder. Now he was a maturing young man who, at six-foot-two, stood taller than me. And who, like every single high school senior I've ever known, was champing at the bit to be free of class work and teachers. That meant me.

My duties had almost come to an end. At nineteen, Stevie no longer needed a big brother/father figure controlling his life, telling him how much money he could have, when he could party and when to stay home. Honestly, I was ready for the change, too. I was newly wed and wanted to build a life with my beautiful wife. I'd long been emotionally, mentally and physically depleted by the onion-like layers of management responsibilities that had built up around my role. Now, whenever my phone rang, my first thought was "Oh, damn, not another gig."

Both Stevie and I knew it was time for the cord between us to be cut. Still, I had no idea how painful it would be.

* * *

The last year was difficult for many reasons. But there was one primary cause of my increasing frustration—my ability to do my job was being eroded by both Motown and Stevie. Someone else was now setting studio sessions and appearances without clearing dates with me. Stevie was all for it, but I became more and more irritated. I'd always insisted his education was Job One, but as graduation day came nearer, he often interrupted our school schedule for gigs I'd ordinarily have said no to.

Only once before, on that troublesome trip to Paris when he was fifteen, had Stevie directly challenged my authority as his teacher. Now, in his last year of school, it was happening again. When I pointed out that his class work was slipping so much it could jeopardize his graduation, my words fell on typically deaf teenage ears.

Totally frustrated, I finally called Dr. Thompson at the School for the Blind. In all those years, I'd never had to bring a problem to his attention. Infrequent minor difficulties and any questions that arose were always quickly and pleasantly resolved by Lucy Karner. Lucy had been my braille instructor in college, as well as Stevie's sixth grade teacher. Over the years, she'd been my liaison at the school and grown to be a close friend. Lucy's straight-forward yet humorous method of handling whatever came her way made her Dr. Thompson's official unofficial adjutant. The fact that I was contacting him and not Lucy indicated the seriousness of my concern. Dr. Thompson reacted swiftly, telling me to have Stevie in Lansing the next day.

Dr. Thompson deftly managed his mantle of authority without being authoritarian. We met over lunch, where he and Lucy casually chatted with us about all the projects distracting Stevie from his schooling. Stevie enjoyed the adult-to-adult manner of the meeting. But when Dr. Thompson leaned forward over the table and lowered his voice, I also knew Stevie was finally paying attention to the message.

Dr. Thompson laid it right out. "I want you to keep your nose to the grindstone and stay on schedule for the rest of the year or you won't graduate. Ted's been with you now almost seven years. And he wants to finish up and get on with his life."

In the moment of silence that followed, I sensed that Dr. Thompson's words had caught Stevie off guard: *What? Mr. Hull has a life?* I think for the first time he fully considered that I might be more than just an extension of him.

So we were back on track. At least when it came to school. Unfortunately, my management role in Stevie's career continued to spiral out of control.

* * *

After the problems on the trip to Atlantic City and the shows at the Steel Pier in the summer of '66, Esther had finally understood what I'd been trying to convince her of for so long: my responsibilities had grown to be more than one person could handle. As Stevie's stardom grew, so had everything surrounding it—musicians, payroll, expenses, travel arrangements, wardrobe. Having a valet care for Stevie's stage uniforms helped some—although the fellow who'd been hired was so flashy himself, it was sometimes hard to tell who was the star. Yet he was also someone else for me to manage. There were too many details and personalities to handle without assistance. And I literally had no life of my own. If we weren't at the school or on the gigs during the week, then on the weekends we were on the road.

Still, it was months before Motown finally gave us a road manager. While the search was on, I assumed that since I'd practically run the Stevie Wonder "operation" for six years, I'd be involved in the hiring of someone for me to delegate responsibility to, and who would report to me. Wrong. What I got was another boss. A manipulative kid named Don Hunter was hired as Stevie's autonomous road manager. I had nothing to say about anything he did. All of a sudden, I was forced to clear everything I did through him, justifying every expense, decision and timetable. Hunter and Stevie seemed to like each other and I think Stevie was glad to have me pushed from the picture a bit. But Hunter and I didn't get along at all. As far as I was concerned, he was overly aggressive and had an over-inflated ego.

What I never understood was why the company hired someone without any input from me, and why they chose someone so insensitive and ambitious. I thought it was very poorly handled from a business point of view. At its root, the problem was that Berry, Esther and everyone had their hands full. The company's rapid growth and phenomenal success was far grater than anyone's wildest expectations, and Motown had few experienced business managers.

I'm sure that when Gordy hired Don Hunter, he thought he'd made a wise choice. I tried giving Hunter a chance. I saw only one benefit to his presence: I'd become increasingly unhappy about being gone all the time, and Hunter did make it possible for me skip occasional road trips.

It took me a while to realize that the guy had a hidden agenda. I began to see that Hunter was insulating Stevie not only from me but from everybody in Motown. Gene Shelby noticed it too, and neither of us knew how he was allowed to get away with it. I was upset enough to have a formal meeting with Esther and Hunter about the situation. But nothing changed because of my complaints.

I think Hunter saw controlling Stevie as a way to become a songwriter and make some money. He and Stevie did write three songs that were released: *You Met Your Match*, *My Girl* and *I Don't Know Why*. What I found particularly interesting was that Motown must have had high hopes for *I Don't Know Why*—it was the A side of the single with *My Cherie Amour*.

But what really blew my blood pressure through the ceiling was discovering that Hunter tried to have me fired.

Stevie was playing a gig at the Green Door in New York City in 1968. Coincidentally, a few faculty members from the School for the Blind were in town for a conference on exceptional children. Mrs. Polzien, the principal, and the teachers knew Stevie from around campus, but this was a golden opportunity for them to see him as a professional artist. I invited them to a show as my guests and they all had a wonderful time.

When we got back to Detroit, Ewart Abner called me to his office. Abner was an exceptionally sharp fellow whose own recording company, Vee Jay, had folded. He'd joined Motown's talent division as vice president, to lighten Esther's heavy load. I figured he wanted to catch up on how the trip went. Instead, I found myself before a one-man firing squad.

Don Hunter had phoned Mr. Abner from New York, saying I'd hosted a large and noisy party at the show and used Stevie's money's to pay for it. I was stunned. It was bad enough that Hunter had called the school principal and three teachers a "rowdy crowd." Much worse was that he'd accused me of stealing from Stevie. There I stood, having to defend my integrity against such unethical charges to Mr. Abner, who was basically unaware of my years of scrupulous conduct and impeccable financial dealings for Stevie and Motown.

To work that hard for all those years and then have this happen angered me. But how I felt about being called on the carpet by Mr. Abner was barely annoyance compared to my rage at Hunter. I hadn't liked him since day one, although I couldn't put my finger on why. Now I knew my instinct was right—he was a deceitful, unprincipled manipulator who'd lie if it was to his advantage. There wasn't much I could do except redouble my efforts to have as little to do with him as possible.

That wasn't too difficult for a few weeks. Stevie and I were on the road and I had plenty of worries about my student's physical and mental health. He'd become more and more distant and distracted. He'd fallen for a darling girl named Angie Satterwhite, his first real love and inspiration for the song *Angie Girl*. He was also dealing with one of the worst things a singer can face: pocketful of contracts and a sore throat that just wouldn't get better. His voice became so hoarse that he resorted to every home remedy anyone would suggest.

And one he tried proved just how superstitious Stevie could be and how naive he still was. While we were in Washington for several shows, one of the band members told him about a "sure cure"—Stevie should fill a sock with table salt and put it on his throat that night when he went to bed. Stevie misunderstood this brilliant suggestion. Instead of placing the salt-filled sock on his neck, he put it in his mouth. The next morning he sheepishly admitted to me that it hadn't worked. After an hour or so he'd taken the sock out of his mouth because he couldn't sleep. After I stopped laughing, I got him to a doctor, and with a prescription his throat was soon healed.

Shortly after this, the Motown Revue headed for Japan. Hunter was along and constantly underfoot, which pretty much ruined the trip for me. During the tour Stevie became more and more withdrawn. We still held class every day and he did little more than go through the motions on his lessons. I knew he was homesick and missed Angie back in California. But I sensed something else building, an unusual wariness I believed Hunter was fueling.

Complicating matters was the pervasive sense of distrust felt by everyone. Motown performers were constantly on edge because of rumors, and the entire nation was in turmoil over civil rights and the Vietnam war. Yet my biggest concern was Stevie.

One afternoon in the Tokyo Hilton lobby (the only hotel that had my initials, TH, on the glasses; I'm embarrassed to confess I swiped six of them!), Martha Reeves and I were waiting to leave for the show. Normally I kept to myself around Martha, but I was so worried about Stevie that I mentioned my concern, and wondered aloud why he wasn't acting like his normal self.

"Well, you *know* why," she said. "Because Motown treats us all like we're stupid."

I didn't say another word. I'm sure she'd convinced herself that was so, and my disagreeing wouldn't have changed her mind. I knew Stevie had problems with Motown, but something else was going on inside him.

I knew the political climate was having an effect on him. Vietnam War coverage, civil rights and peace demonstrations constantly filled the news, both at home and in Japan. The Tokyo airport was a base for U.S. military flights. Our next stop was the Japanese-controlled island of Okinawa, where B-52s were launching bombing missions throughout Southeast Asia from our Air Force Base. The Japanese were wary of Americans, and tension was inescapable on our tour.

One morning in downtown Tokyo I went out sightseeing, walking around acting like my normal, blind-guy self. Apparently, that looked suspicious to authorities. Two men who identified themselves as Japanese plainclothes policemen accosted me several blocks from the hotel. They were polite as they asked my name, where I was from, what I was doing in Japan and how long I'd be in their country. They asked for my passport. When I said I wasn't carrying it, they took me into custody and insisted on accompanying me to our hotel.

I'll admit it was a scary situation. Walking through the hotel lobby, I saw Phil Woolrich, who was in charge on this Revue.

"Phil, these guys are police officers," I said. "They want to go up and see my documents." He just nodded and watched as we got into the elevator.

But Phil didn't trust the men either and followed us up. In my room, he stood by my side to make sure they didn't give me a hard time. The officers looked over my papers, apologized for causing any inconvenience and left. In the back of our minds, Phil and I had wondered if they thought I was a spy. Maybe we were overreacting, but there was a popular saying that reflected the wartime tension: "Just because you're paranoid, doesn't mean they're not out to get you."

By the time we reached Okinawa, Stevie's deepening reticence had me increasingly worried. "I don't know what's going on in your life right now," I told him, "but you're not acting right. You seem to be thinking an awful lot about yourself these days in a way that's not good. You've got to snap out of this and start trusting again."

He was silent for a moment, then nodded. "Yeah, you're right. I'll try."

Later that afternoon, he called and asked me to come to his room. When he opened the door, he held his finger to his lips before I could speak, then leaned forward and whispered, "I want to show you something."

Stevie took me by the hand. Using his leg to guide him along the edge of the bed, he moved to the night table holding the phone. He reached under and pulled something out. When he put it on the palm of my hand, I realized it was a tiny electronic listening device. Somebody had planted a hidden microphone in his room. He took the bug back and silently replaced it under the table, then led me into the bathroom before saying another word. "I just wanted to show you that."

My first thought was Stevie's penchant for pranks. Had he placed it there to pull my leg? My second thought was, who would want to eavesdrop on him, and why? It could have been a "legitimate" plant by the Japanese police or perhaps our own CIA—we were in a war and American artists such as Stevie could have been suspect when traveling in the Orient. But in Japan, unlike in America, electronic bugs were sold right off the shelf, even at the Tokyo Hilton gift shop where Stevie had bought his first battery operated, portable stereo tape recorder. I wouldn't have put it past Hunter, who's room was next door, to have thought he could make use of eavesdropping on Stevie.

I was truly confounded. Knowing how Stevie loved spending hours on the phone, there was only one thing I could suggest. "Now that you know that it's there, don't say anything about anybody. Don't say anything wrong, don't be critical of anybody. Just leave the thing there and be very careful about what you say."

The only positive aspect of the situation was that by showing me the bug, it told me he trusted that I wasn't the one to plant it. I think he wanted me to know he'd been right to feel something suspicious was going on. Back in my own room, I carefully went over every piece of furniture but found nothing. Neither Stevie nor I ever mentioned his discovery to anyone.

I think Stevie's uncertainty about his future was intensifying the problems he was dealing with. He was unsure what he wanted to do after finishing high school. He talked about going to college. I neither encouraged nor discouraged him, but my personal opinion was that he shouldn't.

Knowing Stevie as I did, I thought the idea was mostly a combination of peer pressure and an ego trip. Stevie's best friend from school, J.J. Jackson, was enrolling at Michigan State and several other classmates were going on to college. The ego part, I thought, was wanting the degree, not so much taking the classes. In a casual conversation with Lula, I mentioned that I didn't recommend college, but as graduation day neared, he began telling the press he was enrolling at the University of California to study composing and arranging.

One day that spring Rebecca Giles called, saying Berry wanted me at a corporate meeting. It wasn't unusual, since I regularly represented Stevie at such meetings. As expected, several of the top Motown staff were in Berry's office when I arrived. What surprised me was to find Stevie and his mother there, too. Although there were several issues on the agenda, it quickly became clear that Stevie and Lula had called for the meeting because they were both upset with me.

"Now Ted," Berry said, "Stevie's mom tells me you think he shouldn't go to college. I'm curious why you think that."

I realized Lula had misinterpreted my earlier comments to mean I thought Stevie wasn't smart enough for college. That simply wasn't so. Testing through the School for the Blind showed Stevie to be an average student who, with my individual tutoring, was able to maintain a B average. On paper, his grades indicated he should have no trouble in college. But, in reality, those of us who are average learners must struggle quite a bit to be successful in college even without a visual impairment, let alone a full-time career.

I'd had no idea that college was of such obvious importance to either Stevie or Lula. Once again my position of trust was under question. Yet in another way, I took this as a compliment from Stevie— through my example and effort, he'd developed a love of learning and knew the importance of a good education.

I felt he'd have to choose between college and his career. And I knew which one was going to win. Course work would quickly become unimportant if he tried to have both. In college, you can't tell the prof, "Well, I'll do this on the go." Stevie would have to be there, in class, not fitting assignments around studio time and gigs the way we did.

"Berry," I said, "Stevie could drop out of this business, go to college and then look for a job. Or, he can forget about college for right now, save that for later on in life, and right now become a millionaire in show business."

As I explained my reasoning, Berry fully understood what I was saying. Commitment to a college degree could mean the end of Stevie's career. There'd be no guarantee he'd return to success after four or more years away from the public. And what opportunities would college equip him for than he had already?

I wasn't sure if Stevie and Lula fully accepted what I was saying, but I think Stevie began to consider the weight of his decision. He ultimately stayed with his career, and has since received several honorary doctorates for work far more important than anything he'd ever have accomplished as a college student.

The college issue wasn't the only reason Stevie was annoyed with me, though. Next on the meeting agenda was his displeasure about pocket money. This was nothing new. He'd always complained I was a tightwad about his allowance, which over the years had doubled—to five dollars a week. I still insisted he didn't need more. We were on the road all the time, either doing shows or at school, and all his expenses were taken care of. I was adamant about controlling the money he had to spend because I didn't want him to grow up with champagne tastes. Neither did the Gordy's.

I knew why he was pushing the issue now. He wanted to buy a synthesizer and was hoping Berry would override my veto. This technology was brand new to the music scene, and were enormous pieces of equipment costing thousands of dollars. On top of the expense, I had another concern. With younger siblings at home and his being on the road so much, I didn't think Stevie could take proper care of such an expensive instrument then.

Berry handled this problem smoothly as well. I think he could have been a good teacher, because he often led by example instead of simply decreeing, "This is the way it's going to be." He casually talked about being the president and founder of this company that was now generating millions of dollars in cash flow. He'd always wanted a boat to play on, he said, and had decided it would be great to get one now.

"Funny thing, though," he said, "last week my accountant told me I can't afford it."

Then Berry picked up a letter and read it to us. A woman who owned a record store in Philadelphia had written him exclaiming about the Motown sound, the lyrics and how her customers loved our records. Berry was terrific about listening to the people who were selling and buying Motown's work. He knew those were the people to please. And he was gently pointing out to Stevie that there was a time to not spend money on luxuries, like boats or synthesizers, but to invest it where it was most important.

It wasn't long, though, before Berry did buy Stevie a synthesizer, and he soon was on his way to becoming one of the great virtuosos of the instrument And sure enough, just as I'd worried, Stevie's younger brother Timothy accidentally spilled an entire bottle of Coke all over it, completely soaking all the electronics inside the instrument.

* * *

I knew how badly Stevie wanted to take greater advantage of his financial success, and how much he disliked my saying no to things he wanted. One of the hardest lessons in helping a young person grow is to measure success by what you give to life, not what you buy. Stevie's natural desire to be a good and helpful person was, thankfully, reinforced by accolades and honors he received regularly for his talent and achievements.

Both he and I made a point of saying as often as possible through the media that the only things a blind person needed for success were an education and a chance. No matter what Stevie went on to accomplish in the future, my greatest pride was in the outstanding role model he was to teens and blind people everywhere.

In the fall of 1968, Michigan's Governor William G. Milliken honored Stevie as the state's Disabled Person of the Year. The Lansing Employ the Handicapped Committee had nominated him for the award. My friend Gordon Steinhauer, who headed the Committee, asked my help with the application process. I kept the effort secret until Gordon called to tell me the Commission's decision. When I told Stevie, the smile he wore for days must have left his face aching.

Next, the Committee nominated Stevie for the President's Trophy, the national award presented by the President's National Employ the Physically Handicapped Committee. Again, Gordon and I compiled copies of news articles and letters of thanks sent to him from such wonderful people as Dr. Martin Luther King. For weeks the two of us fine-tuned the pages and pages of material required with the application. We never said a word to Stevie. Off we sent the package to Washington, D.C. As we waited, I worried. Neither Gordon nor I had any idea who else was being nominated. And Stevie's youth might work against his earning such a high honor.

This time, Stevie found out about the award before I did. Esther called one day and breezily asked, "Ted, how'd you like to go to Washington with us when Stevie meets the President?"

Now my pride and happiness was as great as his. But as I'd learned in the Scripture, "Pride goeth before a fall."

Stevie was twelve days shy of turning nineteen when President Richard Nixon presented him with the Distinguished Service Award of the President's Committee on Employment of the Handicapped, one of the greatest honors a person with a disability can receive. The ceremony was held in the White House Rose Garden, where President Nixon told Stevie he "served as an inspiration to all handicapped citizens— particularly the younger ones. You have demonstrated what we mean when we say 'It's ability, not disability, that counts.'"

On hand to meet the President with Stevie were five members of the Lansing Employ the Handicapped Committee, including my buddy Gordon. At Stevie's side stood his deservedly proud mother and Junious Griffin, representing Berry Gordy and Motown. But I wasn't there. Only hours before the event did I learn I wasn't invited. I'd gone up to Stevie's room at the Washington Hilton to make sure he was ready for us to leave for the ceremony. Junious Griffin came in and quickly hustled Stevie out, making it clear I definitely was excluded. Though it didn't diminish my pride in Stevie, I was deeply hurt.

Feeling slighted on such an important occasion only intensified my desire to finish up with this job and get on with my life. I knew Stevie wanted to separate himself completely from me. More and more I was feeling cut adrift from the people I'd worked and lived so closely with for nearly seven years. I knew I'd done a good job and had worked my behind off. As Stevie's graduation day and the end of my job approached, it hurt that nobody at Motown was saying "Doggone, we don't want you to go."

* * *

Twenty-seven students made up the 1969 class of the Michigan School for the Blind. But in the yearbook are pictures of only twenty-six seniors—and the one without a senior portrait is the school's most famous graduate. I have no earthly idea how that one slipped by us. I'm sure we were on the road when the photos were taken. But Stevie got something better—a full-page photo of him at the piano.

The graduation ceremony, on a warm June evening, drew far more interest than any such event in the school's history. The usual roster of Michigan State Capitol politicians in attendance was supplemented by a crowd of people who wanted a chance to see this famous young man. Lansing journalists treated it as media event. All eyes were focused on Stevie Wonder. Still, it was a night of significance for many other reasons.

The President's National Employ the Physically Handicapped Committee awarded the Michigan School for the Blind an "imaginal educational programming award." A proclamation by the Michigan legislature was read by Representative George Edwards, Esther Gordy Edwards own husband. I was honored with a citation from Governor Milliken for the role I'd played in helping the School succeed with the challenge of Stevie's education, one its faculty had never faced before.

Berry Gordy wasn't able to attend the ceremonies. Instead, he sent Ewart Abner, who by then was president of International Talent Management. After the evening's program, Stevie went back to Detroit with his mom. Gene Shelby drove Mr. Abner, and I rode along. On the way, I talked to him about what options might be open for me, either in a new role with Stevie or with Motown.

He understood my concerns and told me he was well aware that I'd done much more than just be Stevie's tutor. He had talked to Stevie and others in the company but no one was considering my continuing with Motown. He was straightforward about the fact that the time was right for Stevie and me to part.

I knew Stevie wanted to be as independent as possible. After all, that meant I'd had succeeded and taught him well. Yet even though I'd always known the day would come when my role in his life would end, the paradox I faced was difficult. I felt I'd made a genuine contribution to Motown. In my heart I knew there was nothing else I wanted to do there or could really succeed at. I was ready to stop being Stevie's tutor and business manager and go on to something else, but after seven years I had no idea what my future held. I wanted to go; I wanted to stay. I was facing a difficult transition filled with conflicting emotions.

I knew Mr. Abner was right, but still wasn't ready to concede there was no future for me at Motown. I wanted to see and talk with Berry.

Berry's busy schedule had always made it difficult for me to meet with him. Early one morning, just moments after my alarm clock went off, Rebecca Giles called. "Berry will see you this morning if you can be at the mansion by 8:30."

Motown owned a mansion not far from the office, in an area of magnificent old homes built by Detroit's early automobile barons. By the 1960s, many of the huge old mansions were turned into apartment buildings because few people could afford to maintain them as private residences. Gordy had bought one to use for business purposes, such as the Sterling Ball, an annual party to raise money for black college students. Often, the mansion served as his second home.

I called a cab and dressed quickly. Following Rebecca's instructions, I had the taxi take me in the back way. One of the servants escorted me to the indoor pool. Berry had just finished his morning swim and was being dressed by his houseboy. Now, I'd seen servants do a lot of things, but never before had I seen a houseboy put someone's socks on for him. I don't know if it was intentional or not, but the message I got was vivid—that Gordy was the rich man and I, in many ways, was the beggar.

George Schiffner, Motown's copyright attorney, was also there. I realized this would be only a token meeting. I did tell Berry how much Don Hunter had interfered with my job. He admitted he'd heard something about my dissatisfaction, but was surprised to learn how much my job had been seriously compromised by Hunter's interference.

We finally got around to discussing what I might do if I stayed with Motown. George asked if I could teach remedial reading, aware, I guess, how badly some of the Motown artists needed it.

"Well, it's not my strong area, unless I can do it in braille." My little attempt at humor was as much a failure as I felt right then, a man without a job surrounded by the trappings of immense power. I felt no jealousy nor bitterness toward either of these wealthy men, but I'd have much preferred to say good-bye to my boss at work, with his sleeves rolled up, instead of watching as a houseboy put on his socks.

* * *

Although graduation day was behind us, Stevie had a few assignments and tests to complete. We continued to meet for class work off and on over the next couple of weeks. But eventually, everything was done. I'd planned no work for the last day of school. Instead, for the couple of hours we were together, we just talked. I'd picked up a copy of a new record, *Switched-On Bach*, and played if for him. It was the first album that used a Moog synthesizer to perform classical music, and I knew he'd be interested in how this new technology was contributing to music.

When the time came for him to go, Stevie said, "I'm sorry about all the b.s. you had to put up with this year." And I knew he honestly was sorry about the problems he'd caused in his desire to be free and spend more time in the recording studio.

"It's okay, Stevie," I told him as he stepped into the waiting cab. "We both lived through it. You've got a great future ahead of you. Things might seem tough sometimes, but remember, you've got a good mind and you can work it through."

Those words had been said to me years earlier by a teacher I greatly admired. In the weeks and months to come, I repeated them to myself often.

The day had finally come. My last paycheck was waiting for me at the office. I'd called ahead to Esther, so I could stop by her office to say good-bye. Our roles within Motown had changed so much over the years that we no longer were as close as we'd once been. I felt that distance when I walked into her office.

"It's good to see you, Ted." Then she quickly added, "I can only spend fifteen minutes. Let's reminisce a little."

As we talked about some of the outstanding experiences we'd been through, my sadness grew, knowing she obviously didn't want to talk about my leaving. We finally said good-bye with a simple, friendly handshake. I headed downstairs to find Gwen Gordy and pick up my pay.

Gwen held out an envelope. "Give me your Motown pass first."

I handed over my company credentials and she gave me my check.

"Bye," was all she said as she turned back to her work.

Inside the office front door, I opened the envelope, only to find more disappointment. After all the years, all the hours I'd invested, my severance pay was only a thousand dollars—before taxes. It seemed almost an insult. I knew that I, and everyone else there, had worked so hard over those years doing our best, often under difficult circumstances, just glad to be part of the phenomenon known as Motown. But what hurt the most was that not one person, not even Stevie, had said "We'll miss you."

I'd lost my job. Even more, I'd lost the boy I'd helped grow into a man. All I could think was, "This must be what it's like going through a divorce or a death. Or the loss of sight."

I walked out of Motown for the last time, into a cool summer rain. For the first time in nearly seven years, no driver waited to take me where I needed to go. And for the first time, I had no place to go except home. In the chilly drizzle, I crossed the street and waited for the bus.

Yester-Me, Yester-You, & Life Today

*"What a temptation for Ted to make himself important,
making Stevie dependent on him. But he didn't. He worked
himself right out of a job. Ted felt like he was losing a son."*
— *Esther Gordy Edwards*

My Wonder years were over.

I really didn't know what I was going to do. The training, the experiences I'd had at Motown didn't equip me for much in the "real" world. At first I didn't worry much, but before long it proved to be a real problem. My experience overqualified me while my education under-qualified me for available teaching positions. And nowhere to be found was anything as exciting as what I had done.

I eventually returned to school, first at Detroit's Wayne State University to earn a certificate to manage sheltered workshops, and then to DePaul University in Chicago for a masters' degree in Human Services Administration. Today, I head the seven-county West Coast Division of Blind Services for the State of Florida, working with visually handicapped adults whose lives are so different from what Stevie Wonder experienced.

I'm often asked if there's been a change in the way we educate our visually handicapped students since the time I worked with Stevie. The answer is yes. And I don't consider them all an improvement.

The greatest change has to in the technology available now for the blind. Computer and printer devices now turn braille into print rapidly, and vice versa. Voice-operated software makes computers more accessible. Inexpensive audio cassette equipment and the rising popularity of audio books bring vast amounts of material to the blind that would otherwise be unavailable or prohibitively expensive in braille. Machines, such as the Kurzweil which Stevie himself helped fund in the 1980s before Xerox took over production, read printed pages aloud through computer-generated voice. Some cities have introduced audible traffic signals. On the market are various canes and specialized eyeglasses, which emit an audible sound when an obstacle appears in front of a blind person.

Such equipment has benefits for certain people under certain circumstances, but in no way do they work well for everyone. For instance, the machines that electronically read print aloud aren't always reliable—the print has to be of good quality for it to be "read" correctly, and they're not reliable with read handwriting or fancy typefaces. No matter what advances technology brings for the blind, braille is still the most efficient way to read and learn.

I don't know any blind person who feels he can rely exclusively on the technologically advanced mobility devices now available. The beeping eyeglasses and canes are easily set off by people or vehicles, which aren't actual obstructions to the blind traveler. The tried-and-true, traditional methods—the white cane, a dog guide and the sighted guide technique, remain the most useful means of independent travel for the blind. Very simply, there is no device on the market that can replace vision.

Yet that day will come. Stevie rocked the world recently when he announced the possibility of receiving a retinal prosthesis. Here, a computer chip is placed on the surface of the retina. Linked to a receptor implant in the brain, information received through the computer chip mimics photoreceptor cell function, and provides very rudimentary visual perception.

If Stevie is a successful candidate for the experimental procedure, it still will not give him perfect vision. His sight would probably be less than mind—at best, he would be able to perceive light and identify shapes and objects.

Artificial vision research has been underway for decades, quietly and with little funding, making slow strides as technology advances. Whether or not this research benefits Stevie, the attention given it by his announcement certainly will have a major impact on the future, and the future of all others who are blind.

Until the day that artificial vision is perfected, special education will remain the most important factor contributing to the success of the blind. Here, many of my opinions are probably viewed as politically incorrect. In principle I agree with the concept of mainstreaming. Normal children who happen to be blind or otherwise disabled should be full participants in the world around them, including school. Unfortunately, this theory too often fails in application, and it's the children who are harmed.

Money for education is so tight everywhere that some counties have only one teacher to work with all the visually impaired students in the district. Children with severe visual impairments are often forced to work with print when they should be taught braille. Because the regular classroom teacher doesn't know or isn't proficient in braille, written communication—the cornerstone of education—is much more difficult. Mobility training is overlooked, or minimal, and extracurricular activities for the blind child are virtually nonexistent.

Few regular classroom teachers have formal training in working with the visually handicapped. As a result, these teachers tend to overprotect the blind child, only reinforcing the child's separateness from sighted classmates. Children are notorious for rejecting peers who are "different," whether it's in physical capabilities or manner of dress. The blind child rarely develops close friendships with sighted classmates and is often excluded from social activities outside of school.

Parents of the visually handicapped who fight for their child's rights make a difference. Those who become active in organizations such as the American Council of the Blind and the National Federation of the Blind help their children learn that blindness does not have to mean dependency. But some sighted teachers and parents, usually with well meant intentions, shield blind their students and children from physical or emotional challenge. "Because you're blind," their attitudes seem to say, "be careful, don't take risks, don't dream. You'll only be hurt or disappointed." Instead of the word, "try," the kids grow up hearing "don't" and "can't"—and soon the world is a place to be feared. Every step of the way through daily life, the message the blind child receive is "You can't ... it's too hard for you." The child translates this as "You're not good enough ... you can't be independent ... you'll never be like everyone else."

Even after all these decades of working with the blind, I don't know which is more difficult to deal with, the adults who hold such misconceptions or the children who grow up thinking that because they can't see, they shouldn't even try to live life to its fullest.

While it is admirable and desirable to mainstream the blind child, a place still exists for residential programs such as the Michigan School for the Blind. Unfortunately, there are fewer and fewer such schools. Just months after the death of Dr. Thompson in 1989, Michigan school the closed due to lack of enrollment and funding. Many residential schools in other states now focus on multiple-handicapped children who, sadly, do not have normal mental capabilities. Fewer and fewer opportunities exist for the average blind child to be fully educated in academic subjects, literary and math braille skills, home economics, shop, physical education and recreation, art, music, and orientation and mobility—all the intellectual pursuits and daily life skills that residential programs provided children like Stevie.

* * *

In the years since we've parted as teacher and student, Stevie's and my lives have taken radically divergent paths. Still, our ways cross occasionally. Margaret and I were proud to attend his wedding to Syreeta Wright in 1970. She was a beautiful, intelligent and talented young woman who collaborated with Stevie on a number of songs, including the hits *Signed, Sealed, Delivered (I'm Yours)*, *If You Really Love Me*,

209

and *Superstition*. It was disappointing, although not surprising, when they divorced in 1972—youth, immaturity, family interference and career pressures had a deadly effect on their marriage.

Shortly after his twenty-first birthday in 1971, Stevie called and asked if he could come by to talk with me. When Gene Shelby dropped him off at my apartment, Stevie was obviously shaken. He told me he'd just left a meeting with Berry and a court representative to take legal possession of his financial account maintained by Motown. After a decade of stardom, he had only $100,000 in earnings. His music had certainly generated substantial profits for the company over those years. He was stunned to learn his share was so small.

Frankly, I wasn't surprised in the least. I'd handled his expenses long enough to know what a huge flow of money it took to make and maintain his career. "If you've got $100,000 in the bank at your age, with the tremendous earning potential you have, you're going to do fine. You've got something that everybody would like to have."

I told him he was expecting way too much. What I didn't tell him was that, in my circumstances, I had a hard time feeling sorry for him. Margaret and I were struggling financially, I was back in school again and our first child was on the way. Stevie was on his way to negotiating a new Motown contract that gave him thirteen million dollars. To me, that sounded like nothing to complain about at all.

Lula Mae and I stayed in touch, too. One afternoon in 1973, during the time Stevie worked so diligently to have Dr. Martin Luther King's birthday proclaimed a national holiday, she phoned, terribly upset. I was extremely concerned and immediately called a cab. At her house I found her in tears, nearly hysterical. Somehow, her phone number had gotten out and she'd been receiving obscene hate calls about Stevie and his latest album, *Living For the City*. Lula isn't the sort to put up with trouble from anyone, but I understood how she couldn't cope with such viciousness directed at her son. I put my arm around her and offered what comfort I could, reminding her that stars like Stevie often pay such an unfair price for their fame. By the time I left, Lula was feeling better. I felt good, too, knowing she still trusted me enough to call in a time of need.

Some years, such as 1976, brought Stevie and me together more often than others. When his schedule made it impossible to personally accept several awards he'd receive at the televised American Music Awards show, he asked Esther and me to attend on his behalf. A few months later he called again, asking my help in pulling a prank on his old school friend J.J. Jackson in Lansing as part of a surprise birthday party. And, before the year ended, Stevie dedicated a new building for the handicapped that I'd developed in Caro, a small town not far away from Saginaw, where he'd been born.

In the summer of 1987, Stevie made his last visit the School for the Blind. The school had been designated as a Michigan historical site and Stevie was the program's guest speaker. The night before, he was appearing at Detroit's Joe Louis Arena and invited me to attend. During the show, he introduced me from the audience and spent about ten minutes joking about our years together. Backstage later, Esther Edwards joined us for a visit.

"Stevie," she said, "you ought to just take Ted with you to the School for the Blind tomorrow."

He thought it was a great idea. But, totally unaware of the reason for his visit, I politely declined. What a disappointment it was to learn weeks later that I'd missed such an important event at the place that had figured so large in both our lives.

The last time I saw Stevie in performance was at the Fox Theater in Detroit in 1988. By then it was fully restored to a glamour and grandeur we'd never known during those early Motown years. Again, he knew I was in the audience and spotlighted and talked about me. Then he dedicated his next song to me—*Fingertips*. At the age of 38, with his incredible vocal range, he still managed to sound almost exactly as he had when we first met.

*   *   *

At Lula's invitation, I had flown to Los Angeles in 1990 to be part of surprise party she planned for Stevie's fortieth birthday. Now, five years later as Margaret and I pulled up in front of 2648 West Grand Boulevard on a May evening, I found myself wishing he would be on hand for this celebration. We were attending the alumni opening of the Motown Museum. Public dignitaries, VIPs, major contributors, politicians and other supporters had attended formal ceremonies a few days earlier. But to me, this night was the truly special one. The only guests were those of us who worked at Motown during all those magic years.

When I walked into the Hitsville lobby, it wasn't at all the same as I remembered. That ramshackle old house was restored to far better shape than I'd ever seen it before. The people (except me, of course) had all changed, too.

A woman stopped me and asked, "Don't I know you?"

"If you worked here," I answered, "I'm sure we know each other."

"I'm Kathleen Anderson," she said with a warm smile and handshake.

I hadn't recognized her at all. Kathy was one of the original Marvelettes, who were cute and sexy and about eighteen years old when I first started at Motown. Now, she was a handsome, mature lady in dignified dress, a formal hat and elbow-length gloves. What had happened to those carefree young people we'd been, I wondered.

After we parted, I went back to Studio A. "Studio A" implied there was a Studio B, but no—Studio A had originally been a single-car garage when Berry first bought the house. There sat the original baby grand piano Ivory Joe Hunter had played during the recording of my song, *Music Talk*. The control room was exactly as I remembered it, right down to the ancient mixing board and two-track taping system. The console, facing the window overlooking the sound studio, was where I'd spent so many hours watching over Stevie during sessions.

Standing there, it was tremendous to recall all the songs I'd seen performed behind that glass. A memory of Stevie doing my song *Purple*

Raindrops surfaced. I'd come into the studio and asked Clarence how it was going.

"Well, it's gonna go okay," he answered, "if I can get The Genie to just sing the melody!" Genie. It was the lighthearted nickname he used when Stevie wouldn't reign in his creativity and do only what Clarence wanted. That "Twelve-Year-Old Genius" I'd taught and helped raise was now a mature man, in complete creative control of his music and the youngest person ever to receive Kennedy Center Honors for career achievement.

Upstairs, Esther's old office was now a photo gallery. As Margaret and I entered the room, the lights suddenly went out. A disembodied voice said, "I apologize, we're having trouble with the wiring."

I couldn't resist adding, "Yeah, and the tour bus used to break down all the time, too."

"Yeah," came an echo I recognized as Joe Billingslea, from The Contours. "And we had to push that sucker after every gig!"

Laughter of shared memories filled the darkened room.

Seeing all the people who were part of that special time in my life reminded me what a unique group we were. These were the studio musicians, the guys who'd worked the sound boards, the gals who'd answered the phones, the people who helped the artists with their costumes and the way they dressed, the way they walked, the way they talked. We weren't the stars, but we were the ones who helped them become stars.

But of the folks I most wanted to see, the ones I'd worked so closely with, only a few were there. Many of the outstanding studio musicians I'd known so well were gone. Jamie Jamerson, the internationally famous bass player, passed away in 1981. Benny Benjamin, the drummer on all of the hits that came out of Studio A, passed on in 1989. Earl Van Dyke, who's keyboard talent made him a nationally famous studio musician, died in 1992. The one death that had hit me the hardest was Clarence's. We'd stayed in touch by phone over all the years and I'd looked forward to seeing him at this reunion. He'd died of cancer just two weeks earlier. Yet Clarence and all the others joined the rest of us in spirit.

Beans Bowles was there. Just as financially strapped as most of us are, his wealth was his historic knowledge of music in Detroit, where he operated the Graystone Jazz Museum. Gene Shelby, who'd been so much more than just a driver to me and Stevie, limped now. He'd lost four toes to diabetes but otherwise was unchanged, still happy and flirting with all the women. Doris Holland, as beautiful as ever, was there—she'd been the original receptionist at Hitsville and had retired only a month earlier. And so was Rebecca Giles, who's still Berry Gordy's personal secretary after all these years.

The champagne flowed freely and elegant hors d'oeuvres filled small plates. It was obvious that over the years these people had learned to enjoy the finer things in life. I thought of how, in the early days, if the choice had been caviar or chittlins, they'd have preferred chittlins any time. But something still told me they enjoyed a good plate of turnip greens and cornbread as much as I.

* * *

It wasn't really until the next day, visiting the Motown exhibit at Greenfield Village, that I was truly swept into the depths of nostalgia.

Entering, I walked into the Motown Cafe. A video narrated by Smokey Robinson delivered a panorama of the people and the Detroit I'd known so well in those eventful years, set against a medley of fabulous Motown hits. It brought tears to my eyes.

In the exhibit was a huge picture of Stevie. I thought back to all the times I'd taken him to Greenfield Village as a student, because it was an excellent place for me to teach history. It had never entered my mind that someday I go back and Stevie would be there, too. If I could have told him then that he'd be a part of history some day, I doubt he'd have believed it.

All I can say, with no greater love and pride than any teacher has ever had for a special student, is that he deserves his place in history. In my heart, and in the world, Stevie Wonder will always hold a special place in the sun.

Printed in the United Kingdom
by Lightning Source UK Ltd.
135414UK00001B/118/A

9 780972 064408